TRE...

A Lesson Commentary for Use with the International Sunday School Lessons

Points for Emphasis
1996-1997

Nashville, Tennessee

© 1996
by Broadman and Holman
All rights reserved
Printed in the United States of America

4217–42
0-8054-1742-7

The Outlines of the International Sunday School Lessons,
Uniform Series, are copyrighted by the Committee on the Uniform Series
and are used by permission.

Dewey Decimal Classification: 268-61
Subject Heading: SUNDAY SCHOOL LESSONS—COMMENTARIES

Library of Congress Card Catalog Number 35-360
Printed in the United States of America

NASB
From the *New American Standard Bible.*
© The Lockman Foundation,
1960, 1962, 1963, 1968, 1971, 1973, 1975, 1977.
Used by permission.

The Scripture used in "The Bible Lesson" is the King James Version.

Table of Contents

- **Introduction** 1

- **First Quarter: God's People Face Judgment**
  ### Unit I: Responses to Wrong
  Sept. 1 — Holding Fast to the Lord 3
  Sept. 8 — Obeying God's Commission 8
  Sept. 15 — Hearing God's Call......................... 12
  Sept. 22 — Proclaiming God's Word..................... 16
  Sept. 29 — Continuing to Trust........................ 20
  ### Unit II: Judah's Internal Decay
  Oct.   6 — A Vain Search 23
  Oct. 13 — False Hopes for Peace 26
  Oct. 20 — A Rebellious People 30
  Oct. 27 — Personal Responsibility 34
  ### Unit III: The Fall of Jerusalem
  Nov.   3 — A Portrayal of Doom........................ 38
  Nov. 10 — Jerusalem Falls............................ 42
  Nov. 17 — A Cry of Anguish 46
  Nov. 24 — God's Power to Restore 49

- **Second Quarter: New Testament Personalities**
  ### Unit I: Persons of Jesus' Nativity and Early Life
  Dec.   1 — Elisabeth and Zacharias 53
  Dec.   8 — Mary, Mother of Jesus...................... 57
  Dec. 15 — The Shepherds 61
  Dec. 22 — The Wise Men and Herod..................... 65
  Dec. 29 — Simeon and Anna 69
  ### Unit II: Persons in Jesus' Ministry
  Jan.   5 — John the Baptizer 73
  Jan. 12 — Mary and Martha............................ 77
  Jan. 19 — Peter...................................... 81
  Jan. 26 — Judas Iscariot 86
  ### Unit III: Persons of the New Testament Church
  Feb.   2 — Barnabas................................... 90
  Feb.   9 — Stephen.................................... 95
  Feb. 16 — Priscilla and Aquila 99
  Feb. 23 — Timothy.................................... 103

■ Third Quarter: Hope for the Future
Unit I: Stand Fast in the Lord
    Mar. 2 — Proclaim the Gospel! 108
    Mar. 9 — Live in Love and Holiness. 112
    Mar. 16 — Pray for Others! 116
    Mar. 23 — Do What Is Right! 120
    Mar. 30 — (Easter) The Resurrection Hope 124

Unit II: Letters to Churches
    April 6 — Commanded to Write 128
    April 13 — To Smyrna and Pergamum 132
    April 20 — To Thyatira 136
    April 27 — To Philadelphia and Laodicea. 140

Unit III: A Message of Hope
    May 4 — The Redeeming Lamb 144
    May 11 — Provision for the Redeemed 148
    May 18 — The Victorious Christ. 152
    May 25 — A New Heaven and a New Earth. 156

■ Fourth Quarter
June: Guidance for Ministry
    June 1 — Christ's Servant Sets an Example 160
    June 8 — Christ's Servant Teaches Godliness 164
    June 15 — Christ's Servant Endures Suffering 169
    June 22 — Christ's Servant Teaches Faithfulness 173
    June 29 — Christ's Servant Encourages Community 176

July, August: A Call to Faithfulness

Unit I: The Greatness of Christ
    July 6 — Jesus Is God's Son 180
    July 13 — Jesus Is Savior 184
    July 20 — Jesus Is the High Priest. 188
    July 27 — Jesus Is the Sacrifice. 192

Unit II: Be Faithful Followers of Christ
    Aug. 3 — Grow in Faithfulness 196
    Aug. 10 — Remain Near to God 200
    Aug. 17 — Remember the Past 204
    Aug. 24 — Renew Commitment 208
    Aug. 31 — Accept Responsibilities 212

■ Alternative Lesson for January 19
    Jan. 19 — Respect for Human Life 216

Introduction
Study to Be Approved!

Bible study can be a habit, a hope, or a hallmark of your life. Sunday School members often attend Bible study as a habit. You get so used to Bible study that you neither expect to get nor actually do get much from it. It remains a habit that makes you feel you accomplished something good.

Often, Bible study is only a hope, a good intention never fulfilled. You keep planning to study the Bible each day or each week, but you know in reality you will do nothing but listen to the results of someone else's study.

For people like my friend John, Bible study is a hallmark. Everyone who knows John knows he studies the Bible daily. How can we tell? Because John describes his Bible study to us? Oh, no. Because John's life shows the marks of the Bible in all that he does and because in life's tough moments, John always has a Bible passage and a Bible truth that guide us to higher ground.

Warning! For this year's study to mean anything to you, Bible study will have to become a hallmark of your life. You will be looking at the dark side of God's work in our history, His judgment on a disobedient people who never gained His approval. You will be looking at Bible characters whose actions may seem strange as in the case of Ezekiel or John the Baptist, depressing as with Judas, or out of your experience as with Simeon and Anna. You are looking at books dealing with deep and demanding concepts as you look at Thessalonians, Revelation, and Hebrews. You will hear God speaking to young pastors and have to apply the truths to your life unconnected with the pastorate.

Daily devotion to God's Word is the way God will speak to you from His Word. Daily devotion is the way Bible study will be the hallmark of your life. Daily devotion is the way you can become approved unto God a workman that needeth not to be ashamed. Hopefully, the points I have emphasized here will help mark the way to a hallmark year for you

Books from BROADMAN & HOLMAN for Studying and Teaching

Laymans Bible Book Commentary,
Volumes 5,11,12,14,15,16,17,18,19,21,22,23,24

The Broadman Bible Commentary,
Volumes 3,6,7,8,9,10,11,12

The New American Commentary,
Volumes 16,22,23,24,26,32,34

Atlas of the Bible Lands,
Larry Thomas Frank, ed.

Old Testament Survey,
Paul R. House

Introducing the New Testament,
Joe Blair

Learning to Study the Bible,
Earl P. McQuay

Holman Bible Dictionary,
Trent C. Butler, ed.

Holman Bible Handbook,
David Dockery, ed.

Holman Book of Charts, Maps, and Reconstructions,
Marsha Ellis Smith, ed.

Pronouncing Bible Names, Expanded Edition,
W. Murray Severance

The Prophets as Preachers,
Gary V. Smith

The Person and Work of the Holy Spirit,
Donald T. Williams

Holding Fast to the Lord

2 Kings 18:1–8, 20:16–21

Why would God let a man like that have children? If ever God needed to step in and stop things, surely that was the time. The man never worked. He made life miserable for his wife and their children. His son had to go to work while still in elementary school to provide finances the father never brought home. What chance did the son have with a father and circumstances like that?—The chance to learn from his father's mistakes. The chance to work his way through college, seminary, and graduate school. The chance to become one of the finest teachers, administrators, and writers I know. The chance to change my life through his friendship.

Lord, increase my faith. You know how to bring hope out of the darkest hours. Help me trust you!

■ THE BIBLE LESSON

1 Now it came to pass in the third year of Hoshea son of Elah king of Israel, that Hezekiah the son of Ahaz king of Judah began to reign.

2 Twenty and five years old was he when he began to reign; and he reigned twenty and nine years in Jerusalem. His mother's name also was Abi, the daughter of Zachariah.

3 And he did that which was right in the sight of the Lord, according to all that David his father did.

4 He removed the high places, and brake the images, and cut down the groves, and brake in pieces the brazen serpent that Moses had made: for unto those days the children of Israel did burn incense to it: and he called it Nehushtan.

5 He trusted in the LORD God of Israel; so that after him was none like him among all the kings of Judah, nor any that were before him.

6 For he clave to the LORD, and departed not from following him, but kept his commandments, which the LORD commanded Moses.

7 And the LORD was with him; and he prospered whithersoever he went forth: and he rebelled against the king of Assyria, and served him not.

8 He smote the Philistines, even unto Gaza, and the borders thereof, from the tower of the watchmen to the fenced city.

....

16 And Isaiah said unto Hezekiah, Hear the word of the LORD.

17 Behold, the days come, that all that is in thine house, and that which thy fathers have laid up in store unto this day, shall be carried into Babylon: nothing shall be left, saith the LORD.

18 And of thy sons that shall issue from thee, which thou shalt beget, shall they take away; and they shall be eunuchs in the palace of the king of Babylon.

19 Then said Hezekiah unto Isaiah, Good is the word of the LORD which thou hast spoken. And he said, Is it not good, if peace and truth be in my days?

20 And the rest of the acts of Hezekiah, and all his might, and how he made a pool, and a conduit, and brought water into the city, are they not written in the book of the chronicles of the kings of Judah?

21 And Hezekiah slept with his fathers: and Manasseh his son reigned in his stead.

THE LESSON EXPLAINED

Faith in Action (18:1–6)

The king is dead. Long live the king! Yeah, but do not expect much from him. Why expect him to be any different than his father. You know about Ahaz. He refused Isaiah's call for faith (Isa. 7). He chose religion, religion like those northern kings: worshiping everywhere and every way, except where and how God said. Why, he even sacrificed his own son to pagan gods. First sign of trouble, he ran to Assyria for help, not to God. Gave Assyria everything the nation owned. He moved God's altar out of the way and built one like the Assyrians' in God's temple. What can we hope for from his son? (Compare 2 Kings 16.)

One generation does not have to suffer for the sins of the father (Ezek. 18), nor does a person have to repeat the father's sins. Hezekiah proved that. He took charge of Israel about 725 B.C. and ruled for twenty-nine years. He let God take charge of him. He destroyed all the pagan altars where his father had worshiped. He even destroyed the brass serpent Moses made while the children of Israel wandered in the wilderness (see Num. 21:9). Why destroy what Moses made? Because the people let it become a religious icon. They trusted more in what human hands had created than in the Creator God who had delivered them from poisonous snakes. Hezekiah said they identified the snake with a Canaanite snake god, Nehushtan. Why did Hezekiah do all this? Simply, he acted like David and trusted God more than any other king. He obeyed God. That is what faith is—trusting God so much that you obey Him.

Faith Rewarded (18:7-8)

God notices faith like Hezekiah's. God acts to show He sees such faith. Hezekiah recognized God at work in the political realm. What Hezekiah tried, God made work. Hezekiah even declared independence from Assyria, and God blessed him. Assyria came and sarcastically demanded surrender. Hezekiah turned to God and His prophet Isaiah for help (chs. 18-19). God rewarded him with victory over all enemies, among them the pesky Philistines to the west.

Faith Tested (20:16-18)

Rewarded faith is not "easy street" faith. Faith proves itself in times of discipline and testing. Hezekiah fell sick,

sick unto death. God let him know the truth (vv. 1–8). He had better be ready to die. Ready? Yes! Willing? No! Faith had trained Hezekiah to face hard times (ch. 19). He had only one weapon to battle death: prayer. He used it mightily. He laid out his whole life before God and asked for deliverance. God gave it. But Hezekiah's faith was not perfect. It needed divine signs (v. 8). It gave in to political temptation to appear macho and powerful before foreign guests (v. 13). This gave God opportunity to speak. Faith's rewards do not last forever. Trust must be in God, not in rewards. Isaiah made that plain. Hezekiah's sons would suffer the consequences of Hezekiah's slide from faith. His foreign visitors would take away all he had shown them.

Faith Accepts God's Word (20:19–21)

Faith learns how to respond to God's messages. The voice of death may bring violent prayer (vv. 1–3). The voice of future judgment stands firm. Faith does not seek relief. Instead faith expresses gratitude for time to enjoy life under God before judgment comes. Sadly, faith does not accomplish all it wishes. Hezekiah learned the lessons of his father's wicked life, but he failed to impress these upon his own son. When death came for Hezekiah, he left all he had to Manasseh. Manasseh left every proven path Hezekiah walked and became the most wicked king Judah ever had. His sins caused Judah's eventual destruction (24:2–4). Faith needs to do more than accept God's Word. Faith seeks also to teach God's Word to the next generation. But faith is never perfect. Hezekiah, Judah's best king, proved that.

TRUTHS TO LIVE BY

Faith flourishes even in times of trouble. Family, enemies, personal health all plagued Hezekiah. Still he obeyed God as no other king had. Trouble tested faith but did not take it away.

Faith can characterize persons of every age. Young king Hezekiah had faith to overthrow the entire religious system his father established. Older Hezekiah had faith to ignore enemy threats. Dying Hezekiah prayed and postponed death. In his last days, Hezekiah gladly accepted God's Word even when it contained judgment.

Faith brings God's rewards. God honors you when you honor Him in obedient faith. Hezekiah received various kinds of rewards: military victory, political success, healing, rebuke for wrong, and escape from immediate judgment. God's rewards will fit the situation you face.

Faith obeys. Hezekiah's life provides one major lesson: Faith goes beyond agreeing with God or with the people of God. Faith acts as God commands. Anything less than obedience is not faith, for faith brings tests. Only obedience passes those tests.

■ A VERSE TO REMEMBER

For he clave to the LORD, *and departed not from following him, but kept his commandments, which the* LORD *commanded Moses.—2 Kings 18:6*

■ DAILY BIBLE READINGS

Aug. 26 — Rabshakeh Mocks the Living God. 2 Kings 18:26–36

Aug. 27 — Rabshakeh Rebuked by God. 2 Kings 19:1–7

Aug. 28 — Hezekiah Prays for God's Deliverance. 2 Kings 19:14–19

Aug. 29 — God Promises to Save Jerusalem. 2 Kings 19:20–34

Aug. 30 — God Heals Hezekiah. 2 Kings 20:1–6

Aug. 31 — The Signs of Hezekiah's Healing. 2 Kings 20:7–11

Sept. 1 — Hezekiah's Great Riches. 2 Chron. 32:27–31

Obeying God's Commission

2 Kings 23:1–8a

JUDGMENT! What images race to your mind? Mine goes to a court where I stood with dear friends as their son faced the judge. A store owner detailed how the son had stolen several inexpensive items from his shop. Parents and son had nothing to say. He had been caught red-handed. The judge had no choice. GUILTY! Son and parents buried their heads in their hands, tears flooding down. But what did those tears mean: "I am hurt and angry. I must suffer," or "I am sorry I did what I did. I will never do it again"? How does God react to human tears? Does the meaning behind the tears affect how God responds?

■ THE BIBLE LESSON

1 And the king sent, and they gathered unto him all the elders of Judah and of Jerusalem.

2 And the king went up into the house of the LORD, and all the men of Judah and all the inhabitants of Jerusalem with him, and the priests, and the prophets, and all the people, both small and great: and he read in their ears all the words of the book of the covenant which was found in the house of the LORD.

3 And the king stood by a pillar, and made a covenant before the LORD, to walk after the LORD, and to keep his commandments and his testimonies and his statutes with all their heart and all their soul, to perform the words of this covenant that were written in this book. And all the people stood to the covenant.

4 And the king commanded Hilkiah the high priest, and the priests of the second order, and the keepers of the door, to bring forth out of the temple of the LORD all the vessels that were made for Baal, and for the grove, and for all the host of heaven: and he burned them without Jerusalem in the fields of Kidron, and carried the ashes of them unto Bethel.

5 And he put down the idolatrous priests, whom the kings of Judah had ordained to burn incense in the high places in the cities of Judah, and in the places round about Jerusalem; them also that burned incense unto Baal, to the sun, and to the moon, and to the planets, and to all the host of heaven.

6 And he brought out the grove from the house of the LORD, without Jerusalem, unto the brook Kidron, and burned it at the brook Kidron, and stamped it small to powder, and cast the powder thereof upon the graves of the children of the people.

7 And he brake down the houses of the sodomites, that were by the house of the LORD, where the women wove hangings for the grove.

8 And he brought all the priests out of the cities of Judah, and defiled the high places where the priests had burned incense, from Geba to Beersheba.

■ THE LESSON EXPLAINED

Hearing The Word (23:1-2)

Can a young kid straighten up what his grandfather took fifty-five years to mess up? Josiah answered I am sure willing to try. Manasseh, his grandfather, ruled fifty-five years, longer than any other king of Judah. The inspired author of Kings crowned Manasseh as the absolute worst of all the bad kings. Manasseh's sin was God's last straw: Jerusalem faced final judgment (2 Kings 21:1). Amon, Manasseh's son and Josiah's father, copied his father's ways, but did not do much damage, for he ruled only two years (2 Kings 21:19-26).

Eight-year-old Josiah ascended the throne of doomed Judah. He refused to walk in grandpa's boots. Rather, he looked back to David as his royal role model and moved straight ahead in David's steps: Do everything God says and nothing else. David prepared for the temple. Josiah repaired the temple. Look what he found! A copy of God's Word. How much of the Old Testament existed as a collection in Josiah's day we cannot say for sure. Josiah's actions show he found at least the Book of Deuteronomy and tried to do everything it said.

There Josiah learned what it meant to make and break a covenant with God. He quickly assembled all the people and let them hear what God said about covenant relationships with Him. Yes, Josiah heard God's Word. He gave all the people the same opportunity. He who does not hear cannot do.

Affirming God's Word (23:3)

Josiah heard the covenant word. He affirmed it. He led the nation in renewing the covenant God had made with Moses (see Exod. 24; Deut. 5:2–3; 7:12; 29:2–3; Josh. 24). Every person agreed: obeying God was the only way to live life. Anything else was not lifestyle; it was death-style. Believe God's Word. Ignore anything else.

Doing God's Word (23:4–8)

Promises come easy. How many times have you told God you would do anything He asked? How long did you keep the promise? Israel had a history of promise-making and promise-breaking. Josiah reversed that history to a history of promise-keeping. Promise-breakers like Manasseh had filled God's temple with items used to worship other gods. (Note that the KJV "grove" in v. 4 is literally "Asherah" and refers to the Canaanite goddess; in v. 6, it is the wooden pole used to represent the goddess.) Josiah destroyed every reminder of false worship, even the priests and priestesses. He heard. He affirmed. He carried out. That is obedience. This is the way to experience a love relationship with God.

■ TRUTHS TO LIVE BY

Obedience is based on knowledge. You cannot do what you do not know. Reading God's Word is the essential first step to doing it. Promise God you will spend thirty minutes each day this week in God's Holy Word.

Obedience begins with a promise to obey. You obey that which you affirm as good, right, and authoritative. You obey when you set out clearly what you think is the right course of action. Write down today what you have learned from God's Word. Make the promise to Him to do what He has shown you is right.

Obedience occurs with action. A promise is not obedience. Obedience is acting on promises. What one act will you take today as the first step in obedience?

■ A VERSE TO REMEMBER

[Josiah] made a covenant before the LORD, to walk after the LORD, and to keep his commandments and his testimonies and his statutes . . . to perform the words of this covenant that were written in this book.—2 Kings 23:3

■ DAILY BIBLE READINGS

Sept. 2 — Josiah Ordered Repair of the Temple. 2 Kings 22:1–7
Sept. 3 — Josiah Received the Book of Law. 2 Kings 22:8–13
Sept. 4 — Josiah Spared from God's Wrath. 2 Kings 22:14–20
Sept. 5 — Josiah Ordered the Passover Held. 2 Kings 23:21–25
Sept. 6 — Josiah's Death. 2 Kings 23:26–30
Sept. 7 — Keep God's Commandments. Ps. 119:1–8
Sept. 8 — Live Righteously. Ps. 119:9–16

Hearing God's Call

Jeremiah 1:4–10, 14–17

Mousy Brannon . . . can God use a mousy person to cause you to hear His call to service? He certainly did. Cool, clear evening in the football stadium in Sweetwater, Texas. City-wide crusade. Mousy preached. God spoke. I ran down the aisle. I had known ever since I could remember that I would be a preacher or a missionary. That night God emphasized beyond a doubt that what I had always sensed was true: He wanted me. The following years have seen me following Him at times, not following at other times. But all of the time the assurance remained. God had called. I had answered. My life's course was set no matter how hard I might try to unset it.

■ THE BIBLE LESSON

4 Then the word of the LORD came unto me, saying,

5 Before I formed thee in the belly I knew thee; and before thou camest forth out of the womb I sanctified thee; and I ordained thee a prophet unto the nations.

6 Then said I, Ah, LORD GOD! behold, I cannot speak: for I am a child.

7 But the LORD said unto me, Say not, I am a child: for thou shalt go to all that I shall send thee, and whatsoever I command thee thou shalt speak.

8 Be not afraid of their faces: for I am with thee to deliver thee, saith the LORD.

9 Then the LORD put forth his hand, and touched my mouth. And the LORD said unto me, Behold, I have put my words in thy mouth.

10 See, I have this day set thee over the nations and over the kingdoms, to root out, and to pull down, and to destroy, and to throw down, to build, and to plant.

14 Then the LORD *said unto me, Out of the north an evil shall break forth upon all the inhabitants of the land.*

15 For, lo, I will call all the families of the kingdoms of the north, saith the LORD*; and they shall come, and they shall set every one his throne at the entering of the gates of Jerusalem, and against all the walls thereof round about, and against all the cities of Judah.*

16 And I will utter my judgments against them touching all their wickedness, who have forsaken me, and have burned incense unto other gods, and worshiped the works of their own hands.

17 Thou therefore gird up thy loins, and arise, and speak unto them all that I command thee: be not dismayed at their faces, lest I confound thee before them.

■ THE LESSON EXPLAINED

God Plans the Call (1:4–5)

"When should I expect God to call me? I want to be sure I am ready and listening. I want to have all the necessary qualifications. I do not want the call to come out of the blue so that I miss it."

Not to worry. God does not work out of the blue. He carefully plans all that He does. Before Jeremiah saw the light of day, God prepared everything for the work Jeremiah would do. God knew the life path He wanted Jeremiah to follow even before his mother became pregnant. God is at work in His world, and He works through people like you and me. He knows your talents, your gifts, and your opportunities. He is planning now for work you can do tomorrow, next week, next year, next century. You can count on God to have you ready for His call. Can He count on you to answer the call and do His work?

We Protest God's Call (1:6)

"I am not ready to hear God's call to service." Too young, too busy, too uneducated—everyone has an excuse not to accept God's call. Jeremiah had the best excuse of all. He was not born when God began to prepare His call, and he was quite young when he heard God's call. Anyone was better qualified than Jeremiah. Moses said the same about himself (Exod. 3:11–4:17); so did Gideon (Judg. 6:15). Samuel learned the proper answer "Speak, Lord; for thy servant heareth" (1 Sam. 3:9).

God Prepares the Called (1:7–10)

Protest proves pointless when spoken to God. He has the power to equip you for any task He calls you to. Too young to gain the audience's respect? The awesome God sends; who could command more respect? No speaking ability? God will speak through you. Afraid of people, especially important people? The all-powerful God stands with you, giving you all the presence and protection you need. Don't know what to say? God provides words when you need them. To sum it all up: God has a mission for you. He makes it quite clear. Jeremiah must determine the destiny of nations, destroying some and building up others. He can do it. God has prepared him for the mission.

God Commissions the Called (1:14–17)

"How can I recognize God's mission to which He calls me? God shows it to you. This you must take on faith and wait for with patience. God used two things Jeremiah saw every day to impress upon him the meaning of his call. The early-blooming almond tree meant God was going to act early or soon to fulfill His word. The boiling cooking pot warned sinful Judah that God would use an unidentified enemy from the north to scald God's chosen nation in punishment for sin. God knew Judah's sins. God would not ignore them as Judah had done. Now the proof came. God issued the call to action with the promise of protection. God sent the prophet to prophesy unafraid of powerful people.

■ TRUTHS TO LIVE BY

God had a plan for you before you were born. Life has meaning because life comes from God, is planned by God, and remains nestled in God's hand. You find meaning in life only when you let God find you and reveal His plan for you.

God equips you to fulfill His plan. Abundance of talents does not determine God's call. God works to show His power, not yours. He will enable you to accomplish His plan in His timing when you make yourself available to Him.

God shows you His purpose. Everyday items gain new meaning when God uses them to let you know His purpose for you. A tree and a cooking pot opened Jeremiah's eyes to God's work for him. Ask God daily to show you where He is at work and what He has planned for you to do in that work.

■ A VERSE TO REMEMBER

The word of the LORD came unto me, saying, Before I formed thee in the belly I knew thee; and before thou camest forth out of the womb I sanctified thee, and I ordained thee a prophet unto the nations.—Jeremiah 1:4

■ DAILY BIBLE READINGS

Sept. 9 — God Creates All People. Ps. 139:13–18

Sept. 10— Israel Forsakes God. Jer. 2:4–13

Sept. 11— God Promises Jeremiah Strength. Jer. 1:18–2:3

Sept. 12— Response of an Obedient Servant. Isa. 50:4–9

Sept. 13 — Jeremiah Encouraged to Persevere. Jer. 15:15–21

Sept. 14— Jeremiah Persecuted. Jer. 20:7–12

Sept. 15— Jeremiah Laments His Birth. Jer. 20:13–18

Proclaiming God's Word

Jeremiah 7:1–15

Awestruck! Beauty beyond belief. Only God could give talent to create such richness of color and magnitude of imagery. God's glory alone could be the reason for such an artistic masterpiece. Thoughts flooded my mind as the stained glass of the European cathedral enthralled my spirit. A look down changed the images and the thoughts. The seats in the mighty place of worship remained virtually empty. Only the few faithful gathered to hear a world-famous theologian preach. Everyone else gawked with that tourist's gaze at stop number eighteen on their ten-day know-it-all, see-it-all tour of Europe. Beauty built for the glory of God had become the latest gawking place for travelers unaware that theirs should have been a pilgrim's journey to see God's working places.

■ THE BIBLE LESSON

1 The word that came to Jeremiah from the LORD, saying,

2 Stand in the gate of the LORD's house, and proclaim there this word, and say, Hear the word of the LORD, all ye of Judah, that enter in at these gates to worship the LORD.

3 Thus saith the LORD of hosts, the God of Israel, Amend your ways and your doings, and I will cause you to dwell in this place.

4 Trust ye not in lying words, saying, The temple of the LORD, The temple of the LORD, The temple of the LORD, are these.

5 For if ye thoroughly amend your ways and your doings; if ye thoroughly execute judgment between a man and his neighbor;

6 If ye oppress not the stranger, the fatherless, and the widow, and shed not innocent blood in this place, neither walk after other gods to your hurt:

7 Then will I cause you to dwell in this place, in the land that I gave to your fathers, forever and ever.

8 Behold, ye trust in lying words, that cannot profit.

9 Will ye steal, murder, and commit adultery, and swear falsely, and burn incense unto Baal, and walk after other gods whom ye know not;

10 And come and stand before me in this house, which is called by my name, and say, We are delivered to do all these abominations?

11 Is this house, which is called by my name, become a den of robbers in your eyes? Behold, even I have seen it, saith the LORD.

12 But go ye now unto my place which was in Shiloh, where I set my name at the first, and see what I did to it for the wickedness of my people Israel.

13 And now, because ye have done all these works, saith the LORD, and I spake unto you, rising up early and speaking, but ye heard not; and I called you, but ye answered not;

14 Therefore will I do unto this house, which is called by my name, wherein ye trust, and unto the place which I gave to you and to your fathers, as I have done to Shiloh.

15 And I will cast you out of my sight, as I have cast out all your brethren, even the whole seed of Ephraim.

■ THE LESSON EXPLAINED

Repentance, Not Religion (7:1–7)

National crisis! What do we do? Good King Josiah, the most righteous king in our history, died in battle. Assyrian power seems to have vanished. Egypt wants to take charge. So does Babylon. What should Israel do? Pay allegiance to Egypt? They defeated Josiah. Or to Babylon? They seem to be the rising power. Or should we declare independence and try to rebuild the kingdom of David? Let's go to the temple and worship. Maybe God will lead us to freedom, power, and glory!

Who's that preaching? Jeremiah the prophet. Watch out. His preaching is dangerous. Listen to that. He says we have to make our ways good. He thinks we are evil. What does he know? We are here worshiping God. What more can he expect? He wants us to change the justice system. He wants us to help the poor, the innocent, the helpless. He wants us to ignore the gods of Egypt and Babylon, even when they force us to set up altars for their gods. What should we do? Life as usual that does not upset the political situation? Or change our way of living like Jeremiah says and trust God with our political situation? What a choice!

Righteousness, Not Riotous Living (7:8–11)

"Does God really see my life? Does He really expect me to obey the Ten Commandments?" Not really, said Israel. Most certainly, said Jeremiah. Worship and riotous living do not go together. Choose your lifestyle, or choose My lifestyle. Don't try to fool Me, either. I am God. I know everything you do.

Ruin Not Reward (7:12–15)

"God does not really mean that. He has to have a people. We are the only people He has. Give us proof, Jeremiah. When has God ever done anything like you threaten?" Take a short trip up through Gibeon and Bethel to Shiloh. See the place where Joshua distributed the land (Josh. 18:1), where Eli and Samuel judged Israel (1 Sam. 1:3). What is left there now? Absolutely nothing! Think God does not mean what He says when He promises a people ruin rather than reward? Jerusalem and this temple will look just like Shiloh. Why? Because you refuse righteousness and repentance.

■ TRUTHS TO LIVE BY

Religion is often enemy number one for God. Worship and being in God's house with people just like you may lull you into false security. You may be trusting temple and tradition when God is calling you to experience Him in obedience.

Right living is more important than right attending. God's people are a covenant people. They respond to God's grace by trusting God to show them the best way to live. They commit themselves to live as God says. They show their love relationship with God by living the life of love He calls for.

Righteous judgment has a long history. Preachers warning God's people away from false security began thousands of years ago. Most often, warnings went unheeded, and judgment followed. Is God using Jeremiah to warn you, your church, your nation?

■ A VERSE TO REMEMBER

Thus says the LORD of hosts, the God of Israel: Amend your ways and your doings, and I will cause you to dwell in this place.—Jeremiah 7:3

■ DAILY BIBLE READINGS

Sept. 16— People Refuse to Obey God. Jer. 7:16–26
Sept. 17— People Will Not Listen to Jeremiah. Jer. 7:27–34
Sept. 18— People Are Stubbornly Unrepentant. Jer. 8:8–17
Sept. 19— Jeremiah Mourns for the People. Jer. 8:18–22
Sept. 20— True Wisdom Is in Knowing the Lord. Jer. 9:2–24
Sept. 21— People Called to Amend Their Ways. Jer. 18:1–11
Sept. 22— The Lord Is the True God. Jer. 10:1–10

Continuing to Trust

Habakkuk 2:1–4; 3:17–19

Graduation from college, a high point of every person's life. Not mine. Graduation day found me unconscious in a hospital bed. A stupid decision I had made led to a car wreck that robbed me of summer plans and especially of graduation. I received my degree by mail. Long summer days in bed followed, with books as my only companion. Lots of time to think. A life crisis: how would I respond to the loss of youthful dreams? The prophet Habakkuk shows how he responded to the loss of religious dreams.

■ THE BIBLE LESSON

1 I will stand upon my watch, and set me upon the tower, and will watch to see what he will say unto me, and what I shall answer when I am reproved.

2 And the LORD answered me, and said, Write the vision, and make it plain upon tables, that he may run that readeth it.

3 For the vision is yet for an appointed time, but at the end it shall speak, and not lie: though it tarry, wait for it; because it will surely come, it will not tarry.

4 Behold, his soul which is lifted up is not upright in him: but the just shall live by his faith.

....

17 Although the fig tree shall not blossom, neither shall fruit be in the vines; the labor of the olive shall fail, and the fields shall yield no meat; the flock shall be cut off from the fold, and there shall be no herd in the stalls:

18 Yet I will rejoice in the LORD, I will joy in the God of my salvation.

19 The LORD God is my strength, and he will make my feet like hinds' feet, and he will make me to walk upon mine high places. To the chief singer on my stringed instruments.

■ THE LESSON EXPLAINED

Asking Is Allowed (2:1–3)

Habakkuk breaks the rules prophets are supposed to follow in doing their job. He gives no call vision, uses hymns and taunt songs instead of sermons, and spends much of his time as a prophet alone on a watch tower waiting for God rather than in the midst of the people delivering messages from God. Most of all, Habakkuk asks God questions instead of giving people answers. The first two questions of protest appear in 1:1–4,12–17. Our passage gives God's answer.

Habakkuk wants to know: How can God allow violence to dominate history? How can God possibly use wicked people like those of Babylon to punish His people Israel? Habakkuk is willing to endure God's scolding and reproof if God will give an answer. God says, Here is your answer, but it is not just for you. Write it for all the people to read easily. Make them remember it, so they will see Me in action when the time comes. It is okay to ask Me questions, just be ready to share the answers.

Faith Is Favored (2:4)

"The just shall live by his faith." Paul picked this up and made it the key verse of his theology (Rom. 1:17; Gal. 3:11; compare Heb. 10:37–38). Humans have questions. We do not understand many experiences of life. We cannot trust our own reasoning or our explanations. What then can we trust? We can trust only God even when He seems to be doing something entirely against His nature as we know Him. We must know that the short run does not reveal God's purposes always, but the long run always does. God fights pride expressed by knowing all the answers. He favors faith that asks Him questions and waits for His answers.

Joy Is Justified (3:17–19)

How can I respond to such a God, a God who allows me to live in the dark about much of history and gives me answers that say God is going to act in His time and I have to trust Him while I wait? Habakkuk surprises us as he shows us how to respond. He sings a hymn (ch. 3) that apparently belonged to the temple collection. He closes the hymn proclaiming his joyous faith even if the present situation is impossible. God may provide no food for the people; still,

Habakkuk will rejoice. Joy is justified because the God who acted in the past will do so again, when He chooses.

■ TRUTHS TO LIVE BY

God wants to hear from you. The darkest moment in life is God's invitation to you to talk to Him. Ask Him whatever question is on your mind. Asking questions is never sin. Refusing to accept and trust the answer is sin.

God expects faith to be faithful. Faith is more than a one-time confession of God's existence or of God's saving act in Christ. Faith is trusting God every day in every circumstance. No condition in life, not even a car wreck that ruins all life's plans, is reason to lose faith. Faith stays faithful.

Joy comes from God alone. The world points to many ways to joy: money, indulgence, addiction, sex, pleasure, gluttony, success. The Bible points to only one source of joy: God. Faith expresses joy in every circumstance of life, not because of the circumstance but because of the God who controls all circumstances. Faith remains faithfully joyous even when darkness colors all of life.

■ A VERSE TO REMEMBER

Although the fig tree shall not blossom, neither shall fruit be in the vines. . . . Yet I will rejoice in the LORD, I will joy in the God of my salvation.—Habakkuk 3:17

■ DAILY BIBLE READINGS

Sept. 23— Why Does Evil Go Unpunished? Hab. 1:1–11
Sept. 24— God Will Not Tolerate Wrongs. Hab. 1:12–17
Sept. 25— Woes of the Wicked. Hab. 2:5–11
Sept. 26— Fate of the Wicked. Hab. 2:12–20
Sept. 27— In Wrath Remember Mercy. Hab. 3:1–8
Sept. 28— God Saves the People. Hab. 3:9–16
Sept. 29— God Is Our Refuge and Strength. Ps. 46

A Vain Search

Jeremiah 5:1–6

"Horror in the Heartland: Oklahoma Federal Building Bombed"

"Militia Movement Thought to Be Growing"

"Sex Inquiries Target 4 Teachers"

"Groups Battling for Scott's Gulf Property"

So read the major headlines on the first two sections of *The Tennessean*, the newspaper I read each morning, as I write this lesson. Must I search in vain for good news? Is there any hope for the world? Is anyone good anymore?

World events made Jeremiah ask the same questions.

■ THE BIBLE LESSON

1 Run ye to and fro through the streets of Jerusalem, and see now, and know, and seek in the broad places thereof, if ye can find a man, if there be any that executeth judgment, that seeketh the truth; and I will pardon it.

2 And though they say, The LORD liveth; surely they swear falsely.

3 O LORD, are not thine eyes upon the truth? thou has stricken them, but they have not grieved; thou has consumed them, but they have refused to receive correction: they have made their faces harder than a rock; they have refused to return.

4 Therefore I said, Surely these are poor; they are foolish: for they know not the way of the LORD, nor the judgment of their God.

5 I will get me unto the great men, and will speak unto them; for they have known the way of the LORD, and the judgment of their God: but these have altogether broken the yoke, and burst the bonds.

6 Wherefore a lion out of the forest shall slay them, and a wolf of the evenings shall spoil them, a leopard shall watch over their cities: every one that goeth out thence shall be torn in pieces: because their transgressions are many, and their backslidings are increased.

■ THE LESSON EXPLAINED

Seek Without Success (5:1-2)

"Find a just person. Yes, just one person who obeys My covenant. Find a faithful person, striving to know and do the truth." Jeremiah's mission resembled Abraham's (Gen. 18). God is ready to pardon, at the least excuse, just one obedient person. One problem: Mission Impossible for Jeremiah. The people say all the right words. In court they make oaths in God's name. Still, Jeremiah can find no one who meets God's criteria for pardon. Judgment must come on a disobedient people.

Sad Over Sin (5:3-5)

Sin saddens those God calls to mission. Jeremiah cried out to God. He knew God looked for truth. He mourned like he was attending a funeral even while the people lived. They had their chance. God warned them. He corrected them. He disciplined them. They responded with deeper rebellion, stubborn babies refusing to do what their Father said or petulant teenagers claiming to know more than the behind-the-times Man ever would.

I see the problem. Looking in the wrong bunch of people on the wrong side of town. I've been among the poor, the ignorant, the uneducated. They do not know any better. Oh, I know God is always on the side of the poor and underprivileged, but He surely does not expect to find His obedient people here. I will go to the other side of town. Yes, here are the "great ones." I'll succeed here. They study history. They know how God has acted in the past. Oh, no! They are worse than the poor. They have broken all ties to God. They depend entirely on their own judgment and their own desires. No hope! No just person. Judgment must come!

Sentence on Sinners (5:6)

I tried. Looked everywhere for someone who knew and followed God's ways. No such person alive. I must pronounce judgment. Everywhere they go, something is waiting to destroy them. God's mind is made up, and rightfully so. They are experts in sin and keep sliding back away from God, never trying to please God. Woe is me, and woe is my people.

■ TRUTHS TO LIVE BY

God searches for obedient people. God is at work pursuing a love relationship with you and all other people. To respond to God in love is to obey. Would Jeremiah's search be more profitable today than in his day?

You cannot plead ignorance. God has worked long and hard to show you His ways and His purposes. You know what God expects. Knowledge is not your problem. Determination and will to obey are. What is your obedience rating? Your stubbornness rating?

Sin's salary is sure. Be faithful to sin, and beware. God is faithful to pay sin's salary: destruction, death. Jeremiah's people found out the hard way. Repent, and you can miss a payday.

■ A VERSE TO REMEMBER

Run ye to and fro through the streets of Jerusalem, and see now, and know, and seek in the broad places thereof, if ye can find a man, if there be any that executeth judgment, that seeketh the truth; and I will pardon it.—Jeremiah 5:1

■ DAILY BIBLE READINGS

Sept. 30 — All Classes Indicted. Ezek. 22:23–31
Oct.   1 — False Teachers. Titus 1:10–16
Oct.   2 — Judah's Ingratitude. Isa. 1:2–9
Oct.   3 — God Unable to Pardon. Jer. 5:7–17
Oct.   4 — God Judges Stubborn People. Jer. 5:18–31
Oct.   5 — God Will Destroy Israel. Hos. 13:4–11
Oct.   6 — God's Punishment for Falsehood. Jer. 6:11–15

False Hopes for Peace

Jeremiah 28:5–14

A young preacher caused my family the most pain we have ever felt. My saintly mother-in-law lay on her death bed, crying from cancer. The young preacher had the answer. If she just had enough faith, God would heal her. I wanted to preach him a sermon, "The Human Race: Death Rate 100%." I refrained. I know not if he ever has learned the lesson. From innocent Joseph praying in prison to Jeremiah not marrying and crying to God for answers to Paul and his thorn in the flesh, people of faith have suffered and eventually died. Preachers should never make promises that go against the way God has always acted with His people.

■ THE BIBLE LESSON

5 Then the prophet Jeremiah said unto the prophet Hananiah in the presence of the priests, and in the presence of all the people that stood in the house of the LORD,

6 Even the prophet Jeremiah said, Amen: the LORD do so: the LORD perform thy words which thou hast prophesied, to bring again the vessels of the LORD's house, and all that is carried away captive, from Babylon into this place.

7 Nevertheless hear thou now this word that I speak in thine ears, and in the ears of all the people;

8 The prophets that have been before me and before thee of old prophesied both against many countries, and against great kingdoms, of war, and of evil, and of pestilence.

9 The prophet which prophesieth of peace, when the word of the prophet shall come to pass, then shall the prophet be known, that the LORD hath truly sent him.

10 Then Hananiah the prophet took the yoke from off the prophet Jeremiah's neck, and brake it.

11 And Hananiah spake in the presence of all the people, saying, Thus saith the LORD; Even so will I break the yoke of

Nebuchadnezzar king of Babylon from the neck of all nations within the space of two full years. And the prophet Jeremiah went his way.

12 Then the word of the LORD came unto Jeremiah the prophet, after that Hananiah the prophet had broken the yoke from off the neck of the prophet Jeremiah, saying,

13 Go and tell Hananiah, saying, Thus saith the LORD; Thou has broken the yokes of wood; but thou shalt make for them yokes of iron.

14 For thus saith the LORD of hosts, the God of Israel; I have put a yoke of iron upon the neck of all these nations, that they may serve Nebuchadnezzar king of Babylon; and they shall serve him: and I have given him the beasts of the field also.

THE LESSON EXPLAINED

Peace, Please, Peace! (28:5-6)

Come one, come all. See the battle of the prophets. Two preachers are going at it toe to toe, Bible verse to Bible verse. In the left corner, Hananiah from Gibeon. He is the people's favorite. You know many of Israel's leaders entered exile in Babylon in 597 B.C. Hananiah promises they will return in two years. That means Jeremiah is wrong. Jeremiah keeps going around with an oxen yoke on his neck symbolizing what God is using Babylon to do to Israel.

Wait a minute. Jeremiah has a reply. Amen, he says. I do wish God would bring your words to pass. They sound so good. They are just what we all want. Oh, that peace could come to Jerusalem.

Prove Yourself, Peace Prophet (28:7-9)

Jeremiah's not through. He wants to teach a history lesson. Think of every prophet you ever heard about. What message did they bring? Look at them: Isaiah, Hosea, Amos, Micah. They all pointed to sin among God's people and to God's judgment. Name an exception. Listen, Hananiah, the burden of proof lies on your shoulders. We wait to see your word fulfilled. Then we will know you are a prophet. Remember Deuteronomy 18:22.

The Prophet with a Prophecy (28:10–11)

Enough words. Time for action in this prophet-against-prophet match. Hananiah makes the first move. He grabs the yoke around Jeremiah's neck. He takes it clear off. He breaks it to pieces. That ought to show Jeremiah. God has not even protected the symbol He gave Jeremiah. Now Hananiah has the symbolic advantage. Just as he broke Jeremiah's yoke, so God will break the yoke the king of Babylon has placed on Judah.

Jeremiah's turn. No action. No words. He turns away. A prophet has no prophecy. What does that say about God?

Pain Not Peace (28:12–14)

God controls prophetic timing and prophetic preaching. The prophet does not. Jeremiah speaks, but only when God gives him the message. Hananiah, you do not know the half of it. You break yokes of wood. Try iron ones. You cannot break those. Nebuchadnezzar, king of Babylon has an iron yoke that fits Judah's neck and that of all the other nations. Why have you tried to make God's people believe a lie? Preach what God says, not what the people want.

■ TRUTHS TO LIVE BY

Short-term profits prove nothing. Peace preachers have plenty of evidence that their message is right. In the short term they can point to healing, money, friendships, influence, popularity, and the inability of other preachers to prove them wrong. Long term shows the difference. When God acts, peace prophets seeking profits find disaster.

God's Word comes in God's time. True preachers face embarrassment. They do not have a word for every occasion. They cannot "out-argue" peace-and-prosperity preachers.

They know their limits. True prophets can speak only after God speaks.

History, not popularity, shows which preacher is right. God works through history. He chooses the historical moment to act. He does not feel it necessary to show which preacher is right at the moment. He waits to find the moment most effective to achieve His saving purposes.

■ A VERSE TO REMEMBER

Then shall ye call upon me, and ye shall go and pray unto me, and I will hearken unto you. And ye shall seek me, and find me, when ye shall search for me with all your heart.
— Jeremiah 29:12

■ DAILY BIBLE READINGS

Oct. 7 — Do Not Listen to False Prophets. Jer. 23:16–22
Oct. 8 — False Prophets Against God. Deut. 13:1–5
Oct. 9 — Do Not Fear False Prophets. Deut. 18:15–22
Oct. 10 — False Prophets Spoke to Exiles. Jer. 29:3–9
Oct. 11 — God Promised to Hear Prayers. Jer. 29:10–14
Oct. 12 — Prophets Are the Lord's Servants. Jer. 29:15–19
Oct. 13 — God Punishes False Prophets. Jer. 29:20–32

A Rebellious People

Ezekiel 2:3-7; 3:4-11

A rebel and proud of it—so I was. Editorials for the college newspaper brought trips to the president's office for criticizing the administration's new pet programs. Disagreement with a professor led to forsaking the nearby seminary for graduate school in another state. Refusal to be bound to one tradition led to doctoral studies in a school outside my denomination. Somehow, this led to service out of the country in Europe for ten years. As a stranger there, I learned to appreciate much that I had rebelled against. Ezekiel faced a people who often viewed him as a rebel. He, however, proclaimed God's viewpoint: they were rebels.

■ THE BIBLE LESSON

3 And he said unto me, Son of man, I send thee to the children of Israel, to a rebellious nation that hath rebelled against me: they and their fathers have transgressed against me, even unto this very day.

4 For they are impudent children and stiffhearted. I do send thee unto them; and thou shalt say unto them, Thus saith the LORD God.

5 And they, whether they will hear, or whether they will forbear, (for they are a rebellious house,) yet shall know that there hath been a prophet among them.

6 And thou, son of man, be not afraid of them, neither be afraid of their words, though briers and thorns be with thee, and thou dost dwell among scorpions: be not afraid of their words, nor be dismayed at their looks, though they be a rebellious house.

7 And thou shalt speak my words unto them, whether they will hear, or whether they will forbear: for they are most rebellious.

4 And he said unto me, Son of man, go, get thee unto the house of Israel, and speak with my words unto them.

5 For thou art not sent to a people of a strange speech and of an hard language, but to the house of Israel;

6 Not to many people of a strange speech and of an hard language, whose words thou canst not understand. Surely, had I sent thee to them, they would have hearkened unto thee.

7 But the house of Israel will not hearken unto thee; for they will not hearken unto me: for all the house of Israel are impudent and hardhearted.

8 Behold, I have made thy face strong against their faces, and thy forehead strong against their foreheads.

9 As an adamant harder than flint have I made thy forehead: fear them not, neither be dismayed at their looks, though they be a rebellious house.

10 Moreover he said unto me, Son of man, all my words that I shall speak unto thee receive in thine heart, and hear with thine ears.

11 And go, get thee to them of the captivity, unto the children of thy people, and speak unto them, and tell them, Thus saith the Lord GOD; whether they will hear, or whether they will forbear.

THE LESSON EXPLAINED

Remind the Rebels (2:3–7)

Listening to God's Spirit makes you different from other people. Ezekiel quickly learned this. A priest exiled in Babylonia in 597 B.C., he must have longed for the temple and a place of service there in Jerusalem. Instead, he heard the call from God's Spirit to minister in the strange, enemy land he occupied. Surely God had calm, soothing words for His people in their seclusion and suffering. Think again.

The Spirit had a special name for Ezekiel: son of man. This underlined Ezekiel as a human being among other humans. He might carry the office of priest or of prophet, but he must listen and work as an equal among his people. He had no authority or prestige that made him better than any one else. As they were, he was a son of man, a person.

The Spirit had a special audience for Ezekiel: a group of rebels who refused to learn from the punishment God gave them. In captivity in Babylon they acted just as badly as they had in Jerusalem. Still, God wanted them to hear His Word one more time. Ezekiel must let them know that God still saw them as rebels needing to change their ways of living. What a fearful task. How would the people react? God said, do not be afraid. Just do the work I give you. If looks could kill, you would die; still, I am present, so do not fear.

Stonehead for Stoneheads (3:4–9)

At least the Spirit prepared Ezekiel for the task. He gave the priest/prophet a head harder than those of the audience. He could win any headbutting contest with them. Thus again, no reason to fear. God could have sent Ezekiel to speak to the Babylonians with their difficult language. Instead, Ezekiel faced his own people in his own language with their difficult wills. Ezekiel had the more difficult job.

Prophet Without Prospects (3:10–11)

One problem for Ezekiel: His audience contained few if any prospects for conversion. They would remain hardheaded and hardhearted. "Never mind! Just preach." Would he have faith to proclaim a word that seemed to return to him empty because no one listened?

■ TRUTHS TO LIVE BY

God knows your heart. Ezekiel's audience were religious people with good reputations in the community. They simply refused in their heart to believe God's Word of judgment and act on it. God did not judge them by their acts of worship and piety. He judged them by their hearts of fear, failure, and faithlessness. What does God see in your heart?

God calls to warn, not to win. God's success is not judged by the number who do what He asks. His success is judged by being faithful to His people and letting them clearly know His ways and His purposes. Does God have a messenger of warning in your church? How do you respond?

God seeks dedication, not despair. Israel in foreign exile hundreds of miles from home had every reason for despair. God used the impossible situation to test their resolve. Could they regain a dedication to Him in exile that they had never known in their own land? Will you let God turn your horrid circumstances into opportunity for new dedication?

■ A VERSE TO REMEMBER

And thou shalt speak my words unto them, whether they will hear, or whether they will forbear: for they are most rebellious.—Ezekiel 2:7

■ DAILY BIBLE READINGS

Oct. 14 — Ezekiel Heard a Voice. Ezek. 1:22–28
Oct. 15 — Ezekiel to Speak to God. Ezek. 3:12–21
Oct. 16 — Wait for God's Timing to Speak. Ezek. 3:22–27
Oct. 17 — God Gave Ordinances in the Wilderness. Ezek. 20:1–13a
Oct. 18 — People Disobeyed Ordinances. Ezek. 20:18
Oct. 19 — Look to the Lord. Mic. 7:1–7
Oct. 20 — Prophets Without Honor in Their Own Land. Matt. 13:53–58

Personal Responsibility

Ezekiel 18:1–5, 7–13, 9–20

Personal responsibility. An easy lesson to write or sermon to preach. I know the subject. But applying it to my life! That becomes hard. Difficulty in people skills . . . procrastination . . . failure to take initiative I should. Sure, I know I should work on some things, but really my parents deserve the blame. Too old when I was born. Moved away from their friends immediately. Worked all the time. No social life, certainly not with friends having children my age. Isolated from people, I had no chance to develop certain skills I would like to have. If Mom and Dad had done it differently, I would be different. Their fault! Then Ezekiel speaks.

THE BIBLE LESSON

1 The word of the LORD came unto me again, saying,

2 What mean ye, that ye use this proverb concerning the land of Israel, saying, The fathers have eaten sour grapes, and the children's teeth are set on edge?

3 As I live, saith the LORD God, ye shall not have occasion anymore to use this proverb in Israel.

4 Behold, all souls are mine; as the soul of the father, so also the soul of the son is mine: the soul that sinneth, it shall die.

5 But if a man be just, and do that which is lawful and right,

. . . .

7 And hath not oppressed any, but hath restored to the debtor his pledge, hath spoiled none by violence, hath given his bread to the hungry, and hath covered the naked with a garment;

8 He that hath not given forth upon usury, neither hath taken any increase, that hath withdrawn his hand from iniquity, hath executed true judgment between man and man,

9 Hath walked in my statutes, and hath kept my judgments, to deal truly; he is just, he shall surely live, saith the Lord GOD.

10 If he beget a son that is a robber, a shedder of blood, and that doeth the like to any one of these things,

11 And that doeth not any of those duties, but even hath eaten upon the mountains, and defiled his neighbor's wife,

12 Hath oppressed the poor and needy, hath spoiled by violence, hath not restored the pledge, and hath lifted up his eyes to the idols, hath committed abomination,

13 Hath given forth upon usury, and hath taken increase: shall he then live he shall not live; he hath done all these abominations; he shall surely die; his blood be upon him.

. . . .

19 Yet say ye, Why? doth not the son bear the iniquity of the father? When the son hath done that which is lawful and right, and hath kept all my statutes, and hath done them, he shall surely live.

20 The soul that sinneth, it shall die. The son shall not bear the iniquity of the father, neither shall the father bear the iniquity of the son: the righteousness of the righteous shall be upon him, and the wickedness of the wicked shall be upon him.

■ THE LESSON EXPLAINED

Proverbs Prove Powerless (18:1–3)

Traditional wisdom, knowledge handed down from one generation to the other, guides life for many people. The Book of Proverbs shows the power of proverbial wisdom. Ezekiel 18 shows that traditional wisdom may lead you astray. Long history showing how children suffered when parents did wrong created the proverb: "The fathers have eaten sour grapes, and the children's teeth are set on edge." Israel then used this to explain why they were in exile in Babylon. It was all Dad and Mom's fault. You cannot escape that easily, countered Ezekiel. You do suffer from things parents did, but your relationship with God is not so affected.

Piety Prevails, Not Parents (18:4–9)

Everyone has a relationship with God, because God created each person. Each relationship is special, individual, and free. No relationship with God is held captive to someone else's relationship, even when that someone else is Mom or Dad. The relationship is a covenant relationship, started because God loves each person, set in place when a person responds to God's love with love, and continued as the person responds to God's continuing love with obedience. Sin makes the relationship go sour. Sin pronounces the death penalty on a person. Such sin is my sin, not someone else's.

Obedience annuls the death penalty, placing God's stamp of life on a person. Obedience is not haphazard guesswork. God has set out the boundary lines for the serious game of life each of us plays with Him (see Exod. 20:17). In Christ God has set up the new covenant, giving you a new heart with the rules of the game inscribed on it. One in love with God obeys and lives, no matter what the previous generation did.

Parents Cannot Prevent Punishment (18:10–13)

Personal responsibility has a tough side. I cannot take responsibility for my children. No matter how deeply I long for them to have a love relationship with God, I cannot create such a relationship. My children must respond to God's love with love and obedience. If they turn away from my wishes and go a different direction, they are responsible before God. They must take His punishment for themselves. All my worry and frustration cannot prevent their punishment. Neither reward nor punishment goes either forward or backward among the generations. The soul that sins, dies. The person who obeys, lives.

Personal Prospects: Life or Death (18:14–20)

You face the decision now. Mom and Dad cannot make it. Your children cannot make it. You must make it. Do you want the life God promises you? Or do you want death? Death is easy: do nothing and receive it. Life is more difficult: you must love God, love strongly enough to obey what He teaches you. Which prospect is yours: life or death? No matter what Mom or Dad did, you can do differently. You are not physiological or psychological slaves to their habits. You are free before God to decide. Life or death?

■ TRUTHS TO LIVE BY

Don't blame your environment. Conditions you live in do not determine who you are. God gave you power to decide for yourself. With God you can become what He made you to be, not what the environment caused you to be.

Don't depend on Daddy. Parents' religion is not good enough for you. You must have your own. Mom and Dad may pray for you each day. Until you pray to God, you still face His punishment. You face eternal death.

Don't presume on God. Proverbial wisdom makes you think God has to act in certain ways. Somehow He owes you rewards, success, life because of who your parents are and where you went to church. God is free from all our rules and all our wisdom. You will be free only when you choose a love relationship in which you freely obey Him.

■ A VERSE TO REMEMBER

The son shall not bear the iniquity of the father, neither shall the father bear the iniquity of the son.—Ezekiel 18:20

■ DAILY BIBLE READINGS

Oct. 21 — Ezekiel Made a Watchman. Ezek. 33:1–9

Oct. 22 — Promise of a Righteous Branch. Ezek. 33:10–16

Oct. 23 — The Righteous Shall Live. Ezek. 33:17–22

Oct. 24 — Righteousness Is Rewarded. Ps. 18:17–22

Oct. 25 — Trust in God. Ps. 3

Oct. 26 — Turn from Sinful Ways. Ezek. 18:21–22

Oct. 27 — Each Person Must Test Own Work. Gal. 6:1–5

A Portrayal of Doom

Ezekiel 4:1–13

The picture will not fade. Almost fifteen years old now, the picture is stamped indelibly on my brain. The nurse led me into the intensive care unit. There lay the man I had adored all my life, my father. Tubes and tapes encapsuled him. Words came slowly, almost silently, and with great suffering. Silence gripped my soul. Death's presence robbed this professional wordsmith of the tools of my trade. Ezekiel portrayed doom even more dramatically and drastically.

■ THE BIBLE LESSON

1 Thou, also, son of man, take thee a tile, and lay it before thee, and portray upon it the city, even Jerusalem:

2 And lay siege against it, and build a fort against it, and cast a mount against it; set the camp also against it, and set battering rams against it round about.

3 Moreover take thou unto thee an iron pan, and set it for a wall of iron between thee and the city: and set thy face against it, and it shall be besieged, and thou shalt lay siege against it. This shall be a sign to the house of Israel.

4 Lie thou also upon thy left side, and lay the iniquity of the house of Israel upon it: according to the number of the days that thou shalt lie upon it thou shalt bear their iniquity.

5 For I have laid upon thee the years of their iniquity, according to the number of the days, three hundred and ninety days: so shalt thou bear the iniquity of the house of Israel.

6 And when thou has accomplished them, lie again on thy right side, and thou shalt bear the iniquity of the house of Judah forty days: I have appointed thee each day for a year.

7 Therefore thou shalt set thy face toward the siege of Jerusalem, and thine arm shall be uncovered, and thou shalt prophesy against it.

8 And, behold, I will lay bands upon thee, and thou shalt not turn thee from one side to another, till thou hast ended the days of thy siege.

9 Take thou also unto thee wheat, and barley, and beans, and lentils, and millet, and fitches, and put them in one vessel, and make thee bread thereof, according to the number of the days that thou shalt lie upon thy side, three hundred and ninety days shalt thou eat thereof.

10 And thy meat which thou shalt eat shall be by weight, twenty shekels a day: from time to time shalt thou eat it.

11 Thou shalt drink also water by measure, the sixth part of an hin: from time to time shalt thou drink.

12 And thou shalt eat it as barley cakes, and thou shalt bake it with dung that cometh out of man, in their sight.

13 And the LORD said, Even thus shall the children of Israel eat their defiled bread among the Gentiles, whither I will drive them.

THE LESSON EXPLAINED

Besiege the Battered City (4:1–3)

He's crazy. The prophet finally has lost his mind. Look at him. He's playing kids' games with blocks and things Mom uses around the house. He's playing army like a young kid. And he wants *us* to watch him. We are supposed to learn something from what he is doing, something about the fate of Jerusalem. That's it. The prophet has joined the enemy. He is using prophetic powers to help the enemy lay siege to Jerusalem and destroy it. What can we do to the mad prophet? We all know God has promised to protect us. We will soon be back in Jerusalem, worshiping. God will defeat Babylon. Ezekiel's mad.

Portray the Punishment (4:4–8)

God, surely you do not want me to do this: lie here on the ground on my side for 390 straight days. How could you expect something like this from me? Yes, I want to obey you, but the people already think I am crazy. I know prophets are supposed to perform symbolic acts. I know the people can understand these things acted out better than just explained with words. But no one's ever had to make such an apparent fool of themselves for so long. Come on, God. Okay, *I* will come on. I will act out the exile right before their eyes. I will show them the price of their sin. What? When I finish the 390 days for Israel, then I have to do forty more days for Judah? You will even strap me down so I cannot possibly turn over. Oh, God, you are punishing our people with a horrible punishment!

Demonstrate the Defilement (4:9–13)

Remember, God, I am a priest. I have kept the law faithfully. I want to stay pure even while I do all this acting that you demand. No! I did not hear right, surely. You are so good to provide food for me for all this time, even if it is such a little bit. But I have to cook it on human excretion! You know that breaks every law you ever set up for a priest (Deut. 23:9–14). You make me ritually impure on purpose. That will be Judah's only option. They will have to become impure to eat. Father, what a punishment. How can we bear it? Oh, I can use cow stuff and not human stuff. That's more like it. That's the normal way of cooking. You do care for me even as I have to carry out this awful prophetic task.

■ TRUTHS TO LIVE BY

God's bad news often precedes His good news. Exiles in Babylon hungered for good news of returning home. God brought news of further punishment and suffering. Good news would come only when they had learned the lesson of bad news.

God's discipline may be duplicated. God sets the time span for our discipline when we refuse to obey Him. We cannot set up rules and say God must quit now. In fact, He can start over again and let us suffer the discipline process more than once. Students who will not learn must repeat the course.

God's promises may not point to prosperity. Judgment is the reverse side of God's salvation promises. If we do not show committed love to God, then He will fulfill the dark side of His promises. Life is not a victory trail for people who refuse to obey God.

■ A VERSE TO REMEMBER

Therefore thou shalt set thy face toward the siege of Jerusalem, and thine arm shall be uncovered, and thou shalt prophesy against it. —Ezekiel 4:7

■ DAILY BIBLE READINGS

Oct. 28 — Ezekiel Ordered to Shave Hair. Ezek. 5:1-4
Oct. 29 — Jerusalem's Fate for Sinning. Ezek. 5:5-9
Oct. 30 — The Lord Speaks in Anger. Ezek. 5:13-17
Oct. 31 — High Places to Be Destroyed. Ezek. 6:1-10
Nov. 1 — The Lord Known by His Judgments. Ezek. 6:11-14
Nov. 2 — Days of Punishment. Hos. 9:1-9
Nov. 3 — God Rejects Israel. Hos. 9:10-17

Jerusalem Falls

2 Kings 24:20—25:1–12

An unforgettable sight! What comes to your mind? Two television pictures dominate my memory: the fall of the Berlin wall and the fall of the Oklahoma City Federal Building. One was too good to be true, the other too horrible. The day came when God no longer sent prophets to warn of judgment's horror. One day almost 420 years after David became king of Israel, David's dreams collapsed in a heap of rubble as the Babylonian army destroyed the city of David. How could God let such horror happen?

■ THE BIBLE LESSON

20 Zedekiah rebelled against the king of Babylon.

....

1 And it came to pass in the ninth year of his reign, in the tenth month, in the tenth day of the month, that Nebuchadnezzar king of Babylon came, he, and all his host, against Jerusalem, and pitched against it: and they built forts against it round about.

2 And the city was besieged unto the eleventh year of king Zedekiah.

3 And on the ninth day of the fourth month the famine prevailed in the city, and there was no bread for the people of the land.

4 And the city was broken up, and all the men of war fled by night by the way of the gate between two walls, which is by the king's garden: (now the Chaldees were against the city round about:) and the king went the way toward the plain.

5 And the army of the Chaldees pursued after the king, and overtook him in the plains of Jericho: and all his army were scattered from him.

6 So they took the king, and brought him up to the king of Babylon to Riblah; and they gave judgment upon him.

7 And they slew the sons of Zedekiah before his eyes, and put out the eyes of Zedekiah, and bound him with fetters of brass, and carried him to Babylon.

8 And in the fifth month, on the seventh day of the month, which is the nineteenth year of king Nebuchadnezzar king of Babylon, came Nebuzaradan, captain of the guard, a servant of the king of Babylon, unto Jerusalem:

9 And he burnt the house of the LORD, and the king's house, and all the houses of Jerusalem, and every great man's house burnt he with fire.

10 And all the army of the Chaldees, that were with the captain of the guard, brake down the walls of Jerusalem round about.

11 Now the rest of the people that were left in the city, and the fugitives that fell away to the king of Babylon, with the remnant of the multitude, did Nebuzaradan the captain of the guard carry away.

12 But the captain of the guard left of the poor of the land to be vinedressers and husbandmen.

■ THE LESSON EXPLAINED

Promised Punishment Prevails (24:20–25:3)

Faithful to the end. The Jews of Jerusalem never could believe what was happening. They just knew God would keep His promise to David and preserve a king in Jerusalem over His people forever. No foreign king could even enter the holy city without permission of the king of Jerusalem. So they broke the covenant. That was only a little matter that could be easily set straight at the next big religious festival. "Look, Egypt has a new, powerful ruler. Hophra of Egypt will help us. We can rebel against Babylon and be free." What happened? Hophra did not help. "For two years the Babylonian army has surrounded the city. We have no food, no water. What can we do? Could those crazy prophets have been right? Should we have listened to Jeremiah and Ezekiel and the others?"

Escape Eludes God's Enemy (25:4–7)

Why is God fighting against us? The Babylonians are surely more cruel and sinful than we ever thought of being. We do not deserve this horrible tragedy. Where are you, God?

Just where I told Habakkuk I would be, using a despicable tyrant to punish My unfaithful people. Just where I told Jeremiah I would be, giving Babylon victory over My disobedient nation.

At least, we will get the king out of here. Then we will have a government somewhere. Oh, no! They caught him. Zedekiah could not escape. He must be God's enemy.

The Temple Topples, Too (25:8–12)

God's house has gone up in smoke. Everything we took pride in, every possession we owned, all gone up in Babylonian smoke. We have nothing left. They're putting chains on our feet, tying us together in long lines. We are marching from Zion to Babylon. We are captured. We go into exile. Only the poor we took so much pleasure in cheating, only they are left in our land.

■ TRUTHS TO LIVE BY

Rebellion's reward is ruin. Our plans are so wonderful. Everything has to turn out right. Until we remember we left out God. Ignoring God guarantees ruin and disaster in God's timing. Where is God in your plans?

God's plans leave no escape hatch. We so seldom believe God will judge us. He is always going to get the other guy. We will find a way to fool God and escape. But one day God will come to us and close all escape hatches. Then what?

Holy places may become wholly destroyed. No place on earth guarantees God's blessings. No matter how many good experiences we have had in a church or a camp or a place of prayer, God can bring judgment if the people of the place lose their faithfulness and love for Him.

■ A VERSE TO REMEMBER

But if ye will not hear it, my soul shall weep in secret places for your pride; and mine eye shall weep sore, and run down with tears, because the LORD's flock is carried away captive.—Jeremiah 13:17

■ DAILY BIBLE READINGS

Nov. 4 — The Reign of Jehoiakim. 2 Kings 24:1–7
Nov. 5 — Second Capture of Jerusalem. 2 Kings 24:8–19
Nov. 6 — The Destruction of the Temple. 2 Kings 25:13–17
Nov. 7 — The Leaders Taken to Babylon. 2 Kings 25:18–24
Nov. 8 — King Jehoiakim Set Free. 2 Kings 25:25–30
Nov. 9 — Appeal to God for Help. Ps. 74:1–11
Nov. 10 — God's Sovereign Power. Ps. 74:12–17

A Cry of Anguish

Lamentations 5:1–10, 19–22

Teaching Psalms in seminary made me an expert in prayer. I especially enjoyed teaching Psalm 137 which asks God to take little babies and mash their heads against the rocks. I waxed eloquent on taking your anger and trusting God with it as the essence of honest prayer. Then strange things happened. I traveled to Poland and saw hungry Christians spend six months' worth of food rations to feed visiting preachers. I saw people in Yugoslavia spend an hour in their worship service praying before the preaching. I saw Christians in Israel pray for people who were persecuting them. Prayer became more than something I practiced somewhat slavishly and taught as an academic exercise. Prayer became real as I saw God meeting desperate needs of hurting people. Lamentations pictures such desperate prayer.

■ THE BIBLE LESSON

1 Remember, O LORD, what is come upon us; consider, and behold our reproach.

2 Our inheritance is turned to strangers, our houses to aliens.

3 We are orphans and fatherless, our mothers are as widows.

4 We have drunken our water for money; our wood is sold unto us.

5 Our necks are under persecution: we labor, and have no rest.

6 We have given the hand to the Egyptians, and to the Assyrians, to be satisfied with bread.

7 Our fathers have sinned, and are not; and we have borne their iniquities.

8 Servants have ruled over us: there is none that doth deliver us out of their hand.

9 We got our bread with the peril of our lives because of the sword of the wilderness.

10 Our skin was black like an oven because of the terrible famine.

19 Thou, O LORD, remainest forever; thy throne from generation to generation.

20 Wherefore dost thou forget us forever, and forsake us so long time?

21 Turn thou us unto thee, O LORD, and we shall be turned; renew our days as of old.

22 But thou has utterly rejected us; thou art very wroth against us.

■ THE LESSON EXPLAINED

Anguish Awaits an Answer (5:1–6)

Poor worshipers stand amazed in the ruins of Jerusalem's once awe-inspiring temple. They have no leaders to help them worship. They cry out in angry anguish the deep feelings of their souls. They forget theological niceties. Impressing other people with their prayers is the farthest thought from their minds.

How could God do this to us? Has He forgotten us, His covenant people? How could He give His city, His temple, His people to hated foreigners? We have lost family. We belong to the poorest classes, those God always protected and told His people to protect. Now, no one protects us. What can we do? We have to do what these foreigners say, and they expect us to work all the time. We tried to get Egypt to help us, and Assyria. Nothing worked. Where are you, God?

Sin's Slaughter Simmers On (5:7–18)

Our parents did it to us. They sinned, and we have to bear the consequences. People we looked down on now rule us. No one helps us. We go out of the city to get food, and lurking enemies try to kill us. Without food, our skin shrivels up and turns dark. No one respects anyone else's rights. Anarchy reigns. Joy and celebrations cease. We are sinners, and the results of sin just simmer around us with no let-up. Help, God!

Has the Faithful One Forgotten Forever? (5:19–22)

God, we do not doubt Your existence. You are the Eternal One, always faithful to Your word. But look at us now! Where are You? Have You entirely forgotten about us? Oh, for the good old days when we were Your people. Cause us to return to You like we were then. We cannot stand the way things are. We see nothing but Your anger and rejection! Do something. Change things. Come to us, Lord.

■ TRUTHS TO LIVE BY

Sin's wages are long lasting. We want to endure God's discipline for a couple of days and turn to something new. God sticks at discipline until we learn our lesson and cry to Him for help with repentance, sincerity, and hope.

Divine silence is not divine absence. Hard times make us think God has deserted us. Often, hard times are God's work of discipline and punishment, His way of calling sinners back to Himself. God is always present. He may just be doing things we do not expect from Him. He hears your anguished cry even if you do not see immediate results.

Renewal depends on God. You must pray for Him to turn you back to Him. He is the One who draws people to Himself. We can never reform ourselves sufficiently to turn back to Him on our own. God brings revival and renewal in His time. Pray for it.

■ A VERSE TO REMEMBER

Turn thou us unto thee, O Lord, and we shall be turned; renew our days as of old.—Lamentations 5:21

■ DAILY BIBLE READINGS

Nov. 11 — Prophet's Lament. Lam. 3:1–9
Nov. 12 — Prophet Bitter Over Conditions. Lam. 3:10–20
Nov. 13 — Prophet Recalls God's Mercies. Lam. 3:21–30
Nov. 14 — Prophet Acknowledges Need for Punishment. Lam. 3:31–39
Nov. 15 — Prophet Examines the Situation. Lam. 3:40–48
Nov. 16 — Prophet Urges Vengeance on Enemies. Lam. 3:55–66
Nov. 17 — Assurance of God's Deliverance. Ps. 13

God's Power to Restore

Ezekiel 37:1–12, 14

Death has established close relationships with me. Five brain concussions, a brother's death when I was only twenty, death of four parents, watching a dear friend wither away to nothing but tubes and tape, and conducting many funerals for God's saints have introduced me to death. Still, I do not like it. Death must have an answer. If not, life is hopeless and without meaning. What can I do and say in the face of death? Ezekiel found an answer.

■ THE BIBLE LESSON

1 The hand of the LORD was upon me, and carried me out in the spirit of the LORD, and set me down in the midst of the valley which was full of bones,

2 And caused me to pass by them round about: and, behold, there were very many in the open valley; and, lo, they were very dry.

3 And he said unto me, Son of man, can these bones live? And I answered, O LORD GOD, thou knowest.

4 Again he said unto me, Prophesy upon these bones, and say unto them, O ye dry bones, hear the word of the LORD.

5 Thus saith the LORD GOD unto these bones; Behold, I will cause breath to enter into you, and ye shall live:

6 And I will lay sinews upon you, and will bring up flesh upon you, and cover you with skin, and put breath in you, and ye shall live; and ye shall know that I am the LORD.

7 So I prophesied as I was commanded: and as I prophesied, there was a noise, and behold a shaking, and the bones came together, bone to his bone.

8 And when I beheld, lo, the sinews and the flesh came up upon them, and the skin covered them above: but there was no breath in them.

9 Then said he unto me, Prophesy unto the wind, prophesy, son of man, and say to the wind, Thus saith the LORD GOD; Come from the four winds, O breath, and breathe upon these slain, that they may live.

10 So I prophesied as he commanded me, and the breath came into them, and they lived, and stood up upon their feet, an exceeding great army.

11 Then he said unto me, Son of man, these bones are the whole house of Israel: behold, they say, Our bones are dried, and our hope is lost: we are cut off for our parts.

12 Therefore, prophesy and say unto them, Thus saith the LORD GOD; Behold, O my people, I will open your graves, and cause you to come up out of your graves, and bring you into the land of Israel.

....

14 And shall put my spirit in you, and ye shall live, and I shall place you in your own land: then shall ye know that I the LORD have spoken it, and performed it, saith the LORD.

THE LESSON EXPLAINED

The State of Death (37:1–3)

A walk in a deserted cemetery introduced Ezekiel to death's stark reality. Death produces nothing to bring cheer and gladness. Death causes flesh to rot and then bones to dry out. Death robs of life, breath, muscles, strength, independence, hope, speech. Death takes away everything we hold dear as the powers of a human being. Human beings looking at bones have no hope for them. Death does not suddenly spring to life. Still, God asked, "Can these bones live?" Ezekiel answered correctly: "O LORD GOD, thou knowest." Ezekiel had no reason to think they would live, but he knew he could never sell God short. God could make them live if He wanted to.

The Spirit of Life (37:4–10)

"Preach to dry, dead bones? Why, Lord? Okay, if you say so. Bones, God says breath is coming back in you. Can you believe it?" Israel in Babylon overheard the conversation and wondered what in the world was happening. "Ezekiel knows our nation is dead. There is as much hope for our nation as for these dead bones. We are all dead, never to rise. Look: what is happening? Lot of shaking going on. Skin coming on bones with sinews and muscles. Bones coming together. New people being formed. But they are still dead. No breath in them. What? God wants the prophet to call the winds (Hebrew, *ruach*) so a breath or spirit (both translate Hebrew *ruach*) may come and puff on the dry bones. Look. They live!"

Statement of Hope (37:11–14)

Who is this? What is going to happen now? If dry bones live, then what? The bones are the nation of Israel, the Israel who said all hope is gone. Israel has hope. They will return to their land, to Israel. What does this prove? Yahweh of Israel is the only God. Israel needs to be introduced anew to their God, form a new love relationship with Him, and be His people like never before. But if national resurrection is possible, can individual resurrection be far behind? Hope is never gone, for God has power over death.

▪ TRUTHS TO LIVE BY

Death is your destiny. You cannot escape death. One hundred percent of people die. The question is, are you ready to die? Do you have hope after death? If you have no hope, you are dead already, even if you are breathing.

Life is God's gift. God alone can give the breath or spirit of life. You owe every breath you take to Him. If you are so dependent on Him, do you not need to know Him personally in a love relationship that gives hope for life and in death?

Hope rests in God's actions. Resurrection, life after death, is the only possible way life can have meaning. Humans never have been and never will be able to bring people back from death to full and everlasting life. Jesus Christ shows that God is in the resurrection business. Do you believe He will resurrect you?

■ A VERSE TO REMEMBER

And [I] shall put my spirit in you, and ye shall live, and I shall place you in your own land: then shall ye know that I the LORD have spoken it, and performed it, saith the LORD.
—Ezekiel 37:14

■ DAILY BIBLE READINGS

Nov. 18 — Israel and Judah Reunited. Ezek. 37:15–22
Nov. 19 — They Will Worship One God. Ezek. 37:23–28
Nov. 20 — Israel Delivered from Captivity. Zech. 9:11–17
Nov. 21 — Restoration of Davidic Kingdom. Amos 9:11–15
Nov. 22 — God Redeemed His People. Zech. 10:11–15
Nov. 23 — God Comforted His People. Isa. 49:8–15
Nov. 24 — Sing Praise to the Righteous Lord. Ps. 98

Elizabeth and Zechariah

Luke 1:5–13, 24–25, 59–64

Something different! You have study habits you may not recognize. Nearly every unit of lessons in the Uniform Lesson series takes a concept or theme and studies it through a portion of Scripture for two or more months. The next thirteen Sundays you can kick this habit. We will be looking at personalities in the New Testament. You will enjoy finding how much you are like Bible people, people who knew Jesus or Paul. You will also learn what the New Testament writers want you to learn from the people they write about. Remember, God is the New Testament hero. Everything in the Bible points to God. People are important but not all-important.

■ THE BIBLE LESSON

5 There was in the days of Herod, the king of Judaea, a certain priest named Zacharias, of the course of Abia: and his wife was of the daughters of Aaron, and her name was Elisabeth.

6 And they were both righteous before God, walking in all the commandments and ordinances of the Lord blameless.

7 And they had no child, because that Elisabeth was barren, and they both were now well stricken in years.

8 And it came to pass, that while he executed the priest's office before God in the order of his course,

9 According to the custom of the priest's office, his lot was to burn incense when he went into the temple of the Lord.

10 And the whole multitude of the people were praying without at the time of incense.

11 And there appeared unto him an angel of the Lord standing on the right side of the altar of incense.

12 And when Zacharias saw him, he was troubled, and fear fell upon him.

13 But the angel said unto him, Fear not, Zacharias: for thy prayer is heard; and thy wife Elisabeth shall bear thee a son, and thou shalt call his name John.

....

24 And after those days his wife Elisabeth conceived, and hid herself five months, saying,

25 Thus hath the Lord dealt with me in the days wherein he looked on me, to take away my reproach among men.

....

59 And it came to pass, that on the eighth day they came to circumcise the child; and they called him Zacharias, after the name of his father.

60 And his mother answered and said, Not so; but he shall be called John.

61 And they said unto her, There is none of thy kindred that is called by this name.

62 And they made signs to his father, how he would have him called.

63 And he asked for a writing table, and wrote, saying, His name is John. And they marvelled all.

64 And his mouth was opened immediately, and his tongue loosed, and he spake, and praised God.

■ THE LESSON EXPLAINED

Surprise Visitor (1:5–11)

"I can't wait, Elisabeth. Finally, my day has come. This is one of the two weeks of the year our clan of priests is in charge of the temple. And God let the lot fall on me this time. This is the one time in my life I can enter the holy place, approach the great altar, take away the remnants of past sacrifices, and offer incense on God's altar. Eighteen thousand or more priests, and today God lets me serve His altar."

You certainly deserve it. You have served faithfully all these years. Even if God has chosen not to give us a child, you have done everything He asked. We have had a good life together serving Him. I am so proud of you this day.

What's wrong, Zacharias? Say something! What happened in the temple? Share your joy with me. You want a tablet to write on? You can't speak? An angel surprised you in the temple. That was a shock. No one else was supposed to be there. What happened?

Surprise Promise (1:12–56)

The angel promised us a son? You refused to believe. The angel made you speechless until our child is born?

You could not even share with anyone your experience in the temple?

I am pregnant. The angel's promise is coming true. Our son will be special. After four hundred years God is sending a prophet with His Spirit to His people. He must be preparing for Messiah to come. And we are part of it.

Here's Mary coming to visit. An angel visited her, too. Her son will be the Messiah. Oh, wonderful! Mary, God has blessed you like no other woman.

Surprise Name (1:57–79)

It is time for circumcision to mark our son off as a member of God's covenant people (see Gen. 17). We have waited until this special day to name the child, so everyone can see God's will at work. They are here for the operation. They are naming the child Zacharias after his father. No, oh no. God gave him a name. He is John.

"No one in your family is named John. Zacharias is trying to say something. He's writing. 'His name is John.' Now Zacharias can speak. This is marvelous. God has a surprise for all of us here. We must watch this child. Listen to Zacharias. Prophecy is being fulfilled here, today."

■ TRUTHS TO LIVE BY

God knows your disappointments. Not getting all you want from God is no excuse not to serve Him. God knows what you want. He knows what you and the people of God need to fulfill His purposes. He may have something in store that will chase all disappointment into oblivion. Just wait on Him.

God is at work around you. Prophecy ceased for four hundred years. God did not stop working. Your spiritual climate may look dreary. God has a wonderful forecast and is just waiting to show you His work so you can join in.

God wants you to do things His way. God chose a special name for the son. Obedient parents gave the name despite everyone else's opposition. What do you know God wants you to do even if no one else agrees?

■ A VERSE TO REMEMBER

And they were both righteous before God.—Luke 1:6a

■ DAILY BIBLE READINGS

Nov. 25 — Hannah Prays for a Child. 1 Sam. 1:9–20
Nov. 26 — Hannah's Joy Completed. 1 Sam. 2:1–7
Nov. 27 — Priestly Duties. 1 Chron. 28:28–32
Nov. 28 — Angel Promised Great Joy. Luke 1:14–18
Nov. 29 — Zacharias Struck Dumb. Luke 1:19–23
Nov. 30 — Praise God for His Works. Ps. 111:1–9
Dec. 1 — John Grew Strong in the Spirit. Luke 1:76–80

Mary, Mother of Jesus

Luke 1:26–42

Unique! Nothing like it in history. Never has been. Never will be. Few people, few objects, few events fit the description. Usually we can find other examples that create a category of similar things. Mary, the mother of Jesus, stands out. She is unique. Unique not in who she was by nature but in how God used her for a one-time-in-history event. We can learn much from her without making too much of her.

■ THE BIBLE LESSON

26 And in the sixth month the angel Gabriel was sent from God unto a city of Galilee, named Nazareth,

27 To a virgin espoused to a man whose name was Joseph, of the house of David; and the virgin's name was Mary.

28 And the angel came in unto her, and said, Hail, thou that art highly favoured, the Lord is with thee: blessed art thou among women.

29 And when she saw him, she was troubled at his saying, and cast in her mind what manner of salutation this should be.

30 And the angel said unto her, Fear not, Mary: for thou hast found favour with God.

31 And, behold, thou shalt conceive in thy womb, and bring forth a son, and shalt call his name JESUS.

32 He shall be great, and shall be called the Son of the Highest: and the Lord God shall give unto him the throne of his father David:

33 And he shall reign over the house of Jacob for ever; and of his kingdom there shall be no end.

34 Then said Mary unto the angel, How shall this be, seeing I know not a man?

35 And the angel answered and said unto her, The Holy Ghost shall come upon thee, and the power of the Highest shall overshadow thee: therefore also that holy thing which shall be born of thee shall be called the Son of God.

36 And, behold, thy cousin Elisabeth, she hath also conceived a son in her old age: and this is the sixth month with her, who was called barren.

37 For with God nothing shall be impossible.

38 And Mary said, Behold the handmaid of the Lord; be it unto me according to thy word. And the angel departed from her.

39 And Mary arose in those days, and went into the hill country with haste, into a city of Judah;

40 And entered into the house of Zacharias, and saluted Elisabeth.

41 And it came to pass, that, when Elisabeth heard the salutation of Mary, the babe leaped in her womb; and Elisabeth was filled with the Holy Ghost:

42 And she spake out with a loud voice, and said, Blessed art thou among women, and blessed is the fruit of thy womb.

THE LESSON EXPLAINED

The Preposterous Promise (1:26–33)

Play the three wishes game for a moment: someone promises to fulfill any three wishes you ask for. Everyone plays the game some time in their life. Surely Mary had, too. One wish fleeted across the mind of every Jewish woman sometime in life: could I be mother of the Messiah? A fleeting wish, one no one really expected to happen. But it did happen. God sent Gabriel, the revealing archangel of Daniel 8.

"Who me? How in the world can that be?" questioned Mary.

"No need to fear," replied Gabriel. "You are experiencing God's grace. I know you are a virgin. You have never slept with a man. You are about to marry Joseph. You will not sleep with him, either. Still, you will become pregnant and have a son. You will name Him Jesus. He will be God's Son, the promised king to rule on David's throne forever."

The Perplexed Plea (1:34–38)

"Such things don't happen. I can't be pregnant. I've never been with a man."

"This is not human work. This is the work of God's Spirit. Trust Him. Yes, that is what I said. In a mystical way you will never understand, you are going to be the mother of God's Son. Still having trouble believing this marvelous news? Go see your cousin Elizabeth. Just as you are young, she is old, too old she thinks to have a child. But she is pregnant! With God nothing is impossible! Can you believe that?"

"Whatever you say! I am God's servant."

The Affectionate Affirmation (1:39–45)

"God promised a sign. I will go see Elizabeth."

"Mary! Something strange is happening. You come, and my baby jumps in my womb. God's Spirit is speaking through me. You have even more special news than I have. You are the mother of my Lord. My baby is jumping for joy at your presence. God is rewarding your faith. The angel's words to you will come true. Praise the Lord."

Pregnant Praise (1:46–56)

"The moment comes. All things come together. Reality dawns. God is going to work through me in a way He has never worked before. He is going to fulfill the promises we have all waited for all these centuries. Praise God! Joy in the Lord. Look what He has done for me, for generations of believers, for those who need Him, for our people Israel. The promises from Abraham on, all come together in what God is doing through me. Praise Him!"

■ TRUTHS TO LIVE BY

God works through unexpected people. No one expected God to go to Nazareth to bring the Messiah. Nazareth certainly expected nothing great from mild, meek Mary. God does things His way, putting down the mighty and exalting those of low degree. Are you one God can work through?

God makes the impossible simple. Virgin birth does not happen. Scientifically impossible. Except when God decides to act in a unique way to accomplish His purposes. Are you trying to limit the ways God can work through you? He is in the business of God-sized tasks. Ask Him for one.

The only human response is faith and praise. We spend too much time debating what God might or might not do. God calls us to recognize what He is doing, believe He can and is doing it, and praise Him as He uses us to accomplish His purposes. Praise Him!

■ A VERSE TO REMEMBER

And Mary said, Behold the handmaid of the Lord; be it unto me according to thy word.—Luke 1:38

■ DAILY BIBLE READINGS

Dec. 2 — Accepting God's Plan. Ps. 138:1–8
Dec. 3 — Joseph Accepted Mary. Matt. 1:18–25
Dec. 4 — Mary's Song of Praise. Luke 1:46–56
Dec. 5 — Mary and Joseph Go to Bethlehem. Luke 2:1–7
Dec. 6 — Mary and Joseph Go to Egypt. Matt. 2:13–18
Dec. 7 — Mary and Joseph Go to Nazareth. Matt. 2:19–23
Dec. 8 — Jesus Provides for Mary's Care. John 19:23–27

The Shepherds

Luke 2:8–20

Ordinary night. Work over for the day, so I had a few quiet moments with the family before bedtime. Phone rang. "This is Ernest Hollaway from Nashville. Would like for you to come talk to us about working here?"

Ordinary became extraordinary. Would God call a professor to leave the ivory towers to become an editor? A missionary to leave the foreign field working with over thirty nationalities to return to the homeland? Seemed like a strange way for God to work. Fifteen years later it does not look so strange, for the call to homeland was a call to work with and learn from Herschel Hobbs, to produce *UltraThin Bibles*, *Disciple's Study Bible*, *Holman Bible Dictionary*, *Holman Bible Handbook*, *Holman Book of Biblical Charts, Maps, and Reconstructions*, *Experiencing God Bible*, and, of course, *Points for Emphasis*.

Similarly, shepherds content to stay with the animals in the fields heard God's call to the city, but for a far larger mission.

■ THE BIBLE LESSON

8 And there were in the same country shepherds abiding in the field, keeping watch over their flock by night.

9 And, lo, the angel of the Lord came upon them, and the glory of the Lord shone round about them: and they were sore afraid.

10 And the angel said unto them, Fear not: for, behold, I bring you good tidings of great joy, which shall be to all people.

11 For unto you is born this day in the city of David a Saviour, which is Christ the Lord.

12 And this shall be a sign unto you; Ye shall find the babe wrapped in swaddling clothes, lying in a manger.

13 And suddenly there was with the angel a multitude of the heavenly host praising God, and saying,

14 Glory to God in the highest, and on earth peace, good will toward men.

15 And it came to pass, as the angels were gone away from them into heaven, the shepherds said one to another, Let us now go even unto Bethlehem, and see this thing which is come to pass, which the Lord hath made known unto us.

16 And they came with haste, and found Mary, and Joseph, and the babe lying in a manger.

17 And when they had seen it, they made known abroad the saying which was told them concerning this child.

18 And all they that heard it wondered at those things which were told them by the shepherds.

19 But Mary kept all these things, and pondered them in her heart.

20 And the shepherds returned, glorifying and praising God for all the things that they had heard and seen, as it was told unto them.

THE LESSON EXPLAINED

Taxing Travel and Travail (2:1–7)

Minor, seemingly insignificant roles come to the shepherds. The spotlight focuses on Mary, the baby, and, in its edges, Joseph. God worked out a problem. The baby's mother lived in Nazareth, but prophecy said, "Bethlehem" (Mic. 5:2). God used a Roman emperor to set everybody on the move. Few enjoyed the trip, because it meant registering to pay taxes. Certainly, Mary on the verge of travail had no joy in the journey, especially when the normal sleeping places displayed "No Room" signs. So she bedded down where cattle slept. There God chose to bring His Son into the world.

Remote Revelation (2:8–14)

Who gets to hear the news first? Tough decision, especially when the news is important. God decided to leave the city and enter the remote hillsides with the best news ever announced. "One should not romanticize the occupations of shepherds. In general shepherds were dishonest and unclean according to the standards of the law. They represent the outcasts and sinners for whom Jesus came" (Robert Stein, *Luke*, NAC 24, 108). No one expected shepherds to get the first peek at the Messiah. That could make the Messiah unclean from birth. But that's the way God worked. He sent glorious angels from pure heaven to sinful shepherds among the dirty sheep of earth. Of course, the shepherds froze in fear. The angel responded with salvation: Fear not. I come with joy for you and for everyone. A Savior, the Messiah, the Lord is born. Go to Bethlehem. See Him there. He, like any other baby, will have swaddling cloths, those thin strips of cloth tightly wrapped around His legs and arms to restrict movement and keep the limbs straight. Unusual, however, is His birth place. You should feel comfortable there. He is in a feeding stall for animals. One final good-bye for you from the heavenly choir.

Exciting Excursion (2:15–20)

Used to isolated country life, the shepherds—curiosity aroused, hopes bubbling to the surface—hurried to town, obedient to the heavenly voice. God rewarded their faithful trip. They saw Jesus. Their reactions the Bible does not report. Their actions were important. They became the first missionaries for Jesus, telling everyone about the angels and the Babe. Mary had no guest book for these first visitors, but she wrote their names deep in her own heart. They supplied one more piece of God's wonderful mystery of life for her. They helped her understand who her Child is. Do you understand?

■ TRUTHS TO LIVE BY

Sinners are God's only workers on earth. Judah's leaders categorized people as Pharisees, Sadducees, scribes, sinners. We like to categorize people as saints, normal people, and sinners. God sees all people in one category: sinners. He surprises us because He chooses to call on sinners to do His work. You will never achieve credentials for God to visit you.

God often interrupts you in the middle of business-as-usual. God reserves no special place or time to meet you. He amazes you. He brings the extraordinary in the midst of the ordinary. Are you so tied to daily routine that you miss the divine disclosure?

God makes the wait worth it. Jews, even often-despised shepherds, waited centuries for God to bring the Messiah. When He came, He showed the shepherds unforgettable news. Can you calm your impatience with God long enough to see God at work around you? Will you use His time of silence to prepare to meet Him?

■ A VERSE TO REMEMBER

And the shepherds returned, glorifying and praising God for all the things that they had heard and seen, as it was told unto them.—Luke 2:20

■ DAILY BIBLE READINGS

Dec. 9 — Don't Be Afraid of Adversaries. Isa. 41:11–16
Dec. 10 — Don't Be Afraid of Criticism. Isa. 51:4–8
Dec. 11 — Don't Be Afraid of Changes. Isa. 54:4–8
Dec. 12 — Don't Be Afraid of Adversities. Hag. 2:4–9
Dec. 13 — God Can Free Us from Fear. Luke 12:22–32
Dec. 14 — God Is Our Shield. Gen. 15:1–6
Dec. 15 — Everything, Praise the Lord. Ps. 160:1–6

The Wise Men and Herod

Matthew 2:1–12, 16

He was after me. No intelligence needed to see that. Friends looked to see how I would react. Shock took hold, then fear, then anger. I ran the emotional gamut. My job, my reputation, my life's work and dreams lay on the line. People in power quickly gave advice. In their eyes I had no chance. Quit, run, save your hide while you can. A Higher Power had a word. Now the crisis of belief demanded resolution. Did I have faith in the powers or the Power? I did not have to quit, run, or try to save myself. God's hand did more than I could ever ask. He was only repeating what He has done so many times. The wise men could tell you.

■ THE BIBLE LESSON

1 Now when Jesus was born in Bethlehem of Judaea in the days of Herod the king, behold, there came wise men from the east to Jerusalem,

2 Saying, Where is he that is born King of the Jews? for we have seen his star in the east, and are come to worship him.

3 When Herod the king had heard these things, he was troubled, and all Jerusalem with him.

4 And when he had gathered all the chief priests and scribes of the people together, he demanded of them where Christ should be born.

5 And they said unto him, In Bethlehem of Judaea: for thus it is written by the prophet,

6 And thou Bethlehem, in the land of Juda, art not the least among the princes of Judah: for out of thee shall come a Governor, that shall rule my people Israel.

7 Then Herod, when he had privily called the wise men, inquired of them diligently what time the star appeared.

8 And he sent them to Bethlehem, and said, Go and search diligently for the young child; and when ye have found him, bring me word again, that I may come and worship him also.

9 When they had heard the king, they departed; and, lo, the star, which they saw in the east, went before them, till it came and stood over where the young child was.

10 When they saw the star, they rejoiced with exceeding great joy.

11 And when they were come into the house, they saw the young child with Mary his mother, and fell down, and worshipped him: and when they had opened their treasures, they presented unto him gifts; gold, and frankincense, and myrrh.

12 And being warned of God in a dream that they should not return to Herod, they departed into their own country another way.

. . . .

16 Then Herod, when he saw that he was mocked of the wise men, was exceeding wroth, and sent forth, and slew all the children that were in Bethlehem, and in all the coasts thereof, from two years old and under, according to the time which he had diligently inquired of the wise men.

■ THE LESSON EXPLAINED

God's Ways or Secure Ways (2:1–8)

Whom do you expect to do things God's way? Political advisors of a foreign, pagan king, or the ruler of God's people? The Jewish king Herod (37 B.C.) caused some people to be suspicious, for his family was tied to Idumea (a continuation in some ways of ancient Edom and some Arab states). Rebuilding the temple continued through much of his reign that started in division and contention, led to peace and prosperity before breaking down into intrigue, manipulation, dissension, and depravity. Jesus' birth in the last two or three years of his reign caused crisis. Apparently foreign wise men first broke the news to Herod. Probably from Persia, they combined roles as sources of ancient wisdom, diviners of current activities of the gods, and priests. They watched the heavens for new signs of divine work. Thus they saw the star and followed it to Jerusalem. They expected the Jewish king to know of significant events in his realm. Instead, Herod had to go to his counselors. They searched Scripture. Micah 5:2 pointed them to Bethlehem. Herod pointed the wise men there. Foreign wise men and Jewish king both claimed they wanted to worship the newborn king, but one did so with joy, the other with troubled spirit, one secure in following God's sign, the other fearful for his own power and position.

God's Ways or Foreign Ways (2:9–11)

The stop in Jerusalem may have been unneeded. The star led on to Bethlehem, but God used the stop to test Herod. The foreign kings made no pretense of wisdom or superior culture. They bowed before the Jewish baby and gave Him their most precious treasures, all symbols of royalty. A Jewish king cares nothing for God's king; foreign political advisors recognize His claim to royalty. Whose ways are God's ways?

God's Ways or Political Ways (2:12–16)

Herod said, Come back. God said, Go the other way. Crisis of belief for foreign worshipers. They chose God's way. They bore no responsibility for Herod's ways, ways that led to killing hundreds of innocent children in an effort to secure his throne from God. God knew Herod's ways. He sent Joseph and Mary away with the Baby, recreating Israel's sojourn in Egypt, while Herod executed his murderous plans. The wise men retained their joy. Jesus remained secure. Herod remained troubled, angry, and insecure.

■ TRUTHS TO LIVE BY

God uses the rich and famous to accomplish His purposes. Few in Jesus' day had better press than the wise men of

Persia, admired far and wide for wisdom, counsel, and abilities to read various indicators of the future. They were willing to forsake their fame and position to travel hard, weary miles across wastelands to find, worship, and give royal gifts to Jesus. Are you willing to sacrifice time from work, position, prestige, power for Jesus?

God's ways test human ways. Herod feared for his life and his position. He refused to seek God's ways at all. He had more faith in Rome's ways. What fears separate you from Jesus? Is God giving you a crisis of faith in the face of your fears?

God's ways overcome human ways. Herod thought a reign of terror could protect his throne. Two years later he was as dead as the innocents he destroyed. Herod's name continues to resound with echoes of terror and hatred. The secure Baby's name brings hope, peace, and salvation. Whose ways are you following: human ways of violence or God's ways of peace?

■ A VERSE TO REMEMBER

And when they were come into the house, they saw the young child with Mary his mother, and fell down, and worshipped him: and when they had opened their treasures, they presented unto him gifts; gold, and frankincense, and myrrh.—Matthew 2:11

■ DAILY BIBLE READINGS

Dec. 16 — Prophecy of a Savior. Jer. 23:1–8
Dec. 17 — Prophecy of a Victorious King. Zech. 9:9–11
Dec. 18 — All Kings Will Worship Him. Ps. 72:1–11
Dec. 19 — The Lord Has Done Great Things. Ps. 72:12–20
Dec. 20 — The Messiah Is Born. Isa. 9:2–7
Dec. 21 — Unbelievers Will Bow to Christ. Isa. 60:10–16
Dec. 22 — Present Our Talents to God. Eph. 4:9–16

Simeon and Anna

Luke 2:22–38

Mazy amazes me. Recently, she gave her public testimony in our church, via videotape. Each Sunday she encourages me with the enthusiasm and vigor she displays as she sings in the choir. Whether she has the best voice or the worst, I do not know. Being tone deaf, I am not too concerned with such matters. Wednesday night she faithfully serves on the staff to ensure the supper is ready for us when we come to the various midweek meetings. I know only a small part of the story. Up to now, I have only viewed her from afar. She represents the thousands of senior adults who faithfully join God in His work and faithfully wait for His reward. They follow the footsteps of Simeon and Anna.

■ THE BIBLE LESSON

22 And when the days of her purification according to the law of Moses were accomplished, they brought him to Jerusalem, to present him to the Lord;

. . . .

25 And, behold, there was a man in Jerusalem, whose name was Simeon; and the same man was just and devout, waiting for the consolation of Israel: and the Holy Ghost was upon him.

26 And it was revealed unto him by the Holy Ghost, that he should not see death, before he had seen the Lord's Christ.

27 And he came by the Spirit into the temple: and when the parents brought in the child Jesus, to do for him after the custom of the law,

28 Then took he him up in his arms, and blessed God, and said,

29 Lord, now lettest thou thy servant depart in peace, according to thy word:

30 For mine eyes have seen thy salvation,

31 Which thou hast prepared before the face of all people;

32 A light to lighten the Gentiles, and the glory of thy people Israel.

33 And Joseph and his mother marvelled at those things which were spoken of him.

34 And Simeon blessed them, and said unto Mary his mother, Behold, this child is set for the fall and rising again of many in Israel; and for a sign which shall be spoken against;

35 (Yea, a sword shall pierce through thy own soul also,) that the thoughts of many hearts may be revealed.

36 And there was one Anna, a prophetess, the daughter of Phanuel, of the tribe of Aser: she was of a great age, and had lived with an husband seven years from her virginity;

37 And she was a widow of about fourscore and four years, which departed not from the temple, but served God with fastings and prayers night and day.

38 And she coming in that instant gave thanks likewise unto the Lord, and spake of him to all them that looked for redemption in Jerusalem.

■ THE LESSON EXPLAINED

Waiting for the Promise (2:22–26)

The Bible provides few biographies but many character sketches. Mary and Joseph were pious Jews. They fulfilled all the laws of childbirth, having Jesus circumcised and giving the sacrifices for Mary's purification (see Exod. 13:1; Num. 3:37–48). At the Jerusalem temple they encountered two amazing senior adults.

Simeon and Anna had taken up almost permanent residence in the temple. They maintained personal reputations as holy, dedicated people and waited for God to fulfill His promises to Israel. The Holy Spirit, a special theological theme in Luke's writings, worked in Simeon's life. The Spirit gave Simeon a special promise: before he died, he would see the Messiah. No wonder he greeted each mother bringing a new baby to the temple.

Experiencing the Promise (2:27–35)

The Spirit led Simeon to the temple in a special way one day. As so often, he saw another mother bringing her child to the temple for the purification and dedication rites. The Spirit moved in Simeon's heart. This is different. This is no ordinary baby. This is the One. Simeon praised and thanked God. No more waiting. The promise was here. He had seen God's Messiah. He could die in peace. Salvation would come to his people. Not only to the Jews but to the rest of the world, too. God had provided salvation for everyone.

The parents had few words but glorious memories. Everything happening confirmed God's original promises to them. Simeon prayed for God's special blessings upon them and told them God had a special work for the child, a work that would separate people into two groups, those accepting His salvation and those falling into judgment by neglecting His salvation. Yes, many would see the sign God gave to Israel in Jesus but would not accept it. Even Mary would stumble for a while and not understand the way Jesus carried out the mission of salvation.

Proclaiming the Promise (2:36–38)

God had one more character sketch for Mary and Joseph in the temple. Anna had prophetic abilities to know God's will and proclaim it to the people. Thus, she was a trusted witness. Her age added to the aura of trust she inspired as did her residence in the temple. Just as Simeon finished blessing Mary and Joseph, Anna appeared and saw the baby. She thanked God for the child and then went out to let everyone know that God had done what He promised: redemption was available for God's people.

■ TRUTHS TO LIVE BY

You can trust God's promises. Generations may separate promise and fulfillment, but God is faithful. What He promises, He delivers. Hope in God is not a fantasy to escape reality. It is the reality that makes life worth living and provides salvation.

You reveal your trust through obedience. Simeon and Anna had character. They faithfully lived out what they knew God expected. Everyone could attest that they obeyed God. Years of waiting in vain and even the sadness of personal loss did not weaken their resolve to obey.

You receive the promise in God's way, not yours. Jesus brought salvation to Jew and Gentile. His salvation lasted for eternity but did not bring peace, power, or victory for Israel's armies. Jesus was the expected king, but His Jerusalem throne was a cross, not a royal seat. Are you obeying God and experiencing Him in such a way that you see Him at work even in ways beyond your expectations?

■ VERSES TO REMEMBER

And it was revealed unto him by the Holy Ghost, that he should not see death, before he had seen the Lord's Christ. . . . And she coming in that instant gave thanks likewise unto the Lord, and spake of him to all them that looked for redemption in Jerusalem.—Luke 2:26, 38

■ DAILY BIBLE READINGS

Dec. 23 — Simeon's Wait Rewarded. Ps. 42:1–11
Dec. 24 — Honor Older Widows. 1 Tim. 5:3–10
Dec. 25 — First-Born Son Redeemed. Exod. 13:11–16
Dec. 26 — The Mission of Servant-Christ. Isa. 42:1–9
Dec. 27 — God Destined People for Salvation. 1 Thess. 5:1–11
Dec. 28 — Salvation Through Jesus Christ. Acts 4:5–12
Dec. 29 — A Sure Salvation. Rom. 8:31–39

John the Baptizer

Mark 1:4–11, 14–15; Luke 7:18–23

Name the presidents of the United States from George Washington on. Now name the vice-presidents. Each of us can look back at places where we worked and name "number two" people. Such people often operate the business day by day, make the decisions that determine success or failure. Yet such people seldom gain fame outside the corporation itself. Today's lesson celebrates "number two" people, the second-stringers who do the work and let others have the glory.

■ THE BIBLE LESSON

MARK 1

4 John did baptize in the wilderness, and preach the baptism of repentance for the remission of sins.

5 And there went out unto him all the land of Judaea, and they of Jerusalem, and were all baptized of him in the river of Jordan, confessing their sins.

6 And John was clothed with camel's hair, and with a girdle of a skin about his loins; and he did eat locusts and wild honey;

7 And preached, saying, There cometh one mightier than I after me, the latchet of whose shoes I am not worthy to stoop down and unloose.

8 I indeed have baptized you with water: but he shall baptize you with the Holy Ghost.

9 And it came to pass in those days, that Jesus came from Nazareth of Galilee, and was baptized of John in Jordan.

10 And straightway coming up out of the water, he saw the heavens opened, and the Spirit like a dove descending upon him:

11 And there came a voice from heaven, saying, Thou art my beloved Son, in whom I am well pleased.

....

14 Now after that John was put in prison, Jesus came into Galilee, preaching the gospel of the kingdom of God,

15 And saying, The time is fulfilled, and the kingdom of God is at hand: repent ye, and believe the gospel.

....

LUKE 7

18 And the disciples of John shewed him of all these things.

19 And John calling unto him two of his disciples sent them to Jesus, saying, Art thou he that should come? or look we for another?

20 When the men were come unto him, they said, John the Baptist hath sent us unto thee, saying, Art thou he that should come? or look we for another?

21 And in that same hour he cured many of their infirmities and plagues, and of evil spirits; and unto many that were blind he gave sight.

22 Then Jesus answering said unto them, Go your way, and tell John what things ye have seen and heard; how that the blind see, the lame walk, the lepers are cleansed, the deaf hear, the dead are raised, to the poor the gospel is preached.

23 And blessed is he, whosoever shall not be offended in me.

THE LESSON EXPLAINED

John's Mission (Mark 1:4–8)

Two clear tasks: baptize, preach. John knew his role. He knew the role required something extraordinary to make people pay attention: extraordinary clothing like the prophet Elijah (2 Kings 1:8) and an extraordinary location in the wilderness or desert near the Jordan River. He attracted attention all right. Despite the difficult terrain and travel, crowds poured out to see him. They did more than come. They listened. They turned away from their worldly mindset. They confessed their sins. They let John baptize them with a new kind of baptism. They experienced forgiveness of sins.

Center stage was not John's mission. He pointed the ones he baptized in a new direction: waiting for someone else. Still wet from John's baptism, they needed another baptism, one that gave them the Holy Spirit. The Coming One brought that. But where was He?

John's Master (Mark 1:9–11,14–15)

An extraordinary day came. Jesus approached John. The Man of lowly-regarded Nazareth faced the desert prophet in his animal skins. Number two baptized number One. The reason became obvious. Heavens opened. A dove descended. A voice thundered: This is my beloved Son, in whom I am well pleased. Number two did the work. Number One received the glory. That's how it was supposed to be. Number two left center stage for prison. Number One followed the Spirit to the place of temptation, the place where angels could minister to Him. Then Jesus went to Galilee. He, too, had a mission: preach the kingdom present in Him; call people to repent and believe. Would crowds shift from imprisoned number two to the wandering number One?

John's Mystery (Luke 7:18–23)

Jesus' miracles did indeed draw crowds. They did not equip an army to take over Palestine from Rome. They did not set up a new throne and a new kingdom in Jerusalem. Israel was not saved from foreign rule. Who is this Jesus? Is He really the One to bring the kingdom of God and the salvation of Israel? Or did John point to the wrong person? Is there another? John wanted to know. In Herod's prison, he did not know how much time he had to get an answer. He sent his disciples to find out.

They found what Jesus did but no words answering who Jesus was. John had to decide. Could anyone but Messiah do what Jesus did? Could God send Messiah and do things in ways different from what John expected? Or would Jesus' words offend John? The gospel remains a mystery. God does not give convincing proof that overwhelms your mind. He gives testimony that calls you to decision. Who is Jesus?

■ TRUTHS TO LIVE BY

Number two is okay when Jesus is number One. Competition, success, winning, putting the other person down . . . these are the world's ways. Becoming number two may represent failure. God sets out the spiritual hierarchy with great clarity. Jesus is Lord. We are servants. He is number One and will remain so. Everyone else is number two and has no higher aspirations.

Number two has a clear mission. When Jesus is number One, we have a clear mission: lead people to Jesus. Each has a separate location, separate appearance, separate style. Everyone has the same goal. We want everyone to let Jesus be number One.

Number two has a clear future. The world does not like number two. You may well face ridicule, persecution, or even worse, being ignored. God will never ignore you. He promises eternal life with Him for all His number twos.

■ A VERSE TO REMEMBER

I indeed have baptized you with water: but he shall baptize you with the Holy Ghost.—Mark 1:8

■ DAILY BIBLE READINGS

Dec. 30 — The Ministry of John the Baptist. Luke 3:1–9
Dec. 31 — People Ask for Directions. Luke 3:10–18
Jan. 1 — John's Witness to Jesus Christ. John 1:29–34
Jan. 2 — John Baptizes Jesus Christ. Matt. 3:13–17
Jan. 3 — Jesus Affirms John's Ministry. Matt. 11:7–19
Jan. 4 — People Believe John Was a Prophet. Luke 20:1–6
Jan. 5 — The Death of John the Baptist. Matt. 14:1–12

Mary and Martha

Luke 10:38–42; John 12:1–8

Ina and Juel, sisters, my mother and my aunt. One spent her life in the big city as a business executive. The metropolitan newspaper kept up-dated photos of her and often reported on her business and social activities. Finally, her death made headline news. Her church knew her as a faithful attender who loved her pastor and made substantial financial contributions. Friends knew her as one who quietly lived out her religious beliefs in helping immigrants, mission projects, and people in need. The other sister ended up living life in a small, isolated town, raising two boys, not working outside the home, teaching Sunday School for senior adult women, and visiting tirelessly for the class. Quietly behind the scenes she helped numerous people who could not help themselves. Seldom did the small-town newspaper take note of her. Even her death brought only a small notice. You could fill in your own examples of sisters Opposite. The Bible tells of Mary and Martha.

■ THE BIBLE LESSON

LUKE 10

38 Now it came to pass, as they went, that he entered into a certain village: and a certain woman named Martha received him into her house.

39 And she had a sister called Mary, which also sat at Jesus' feet, and heard his word.

40 But Martha was cumbered about much serving, and came to him, and said, Lord, dost thou not care that my sister hath left me to serve alone? bid her therefore that she help me.

41 And Jesus answered and said unto her, Martha, Martha, thou art careful and troubled about many things:

42 But one thing is needful: and Mary hath chosen that good part, which shall not be taken away from her.

....

JOHN 12

1 Then Jesus six days before the passover came to Bethany, where Lazarus was which had been dead, whom he raised from the dead.

2 There they made him a supper; and Martha served: but Lazarus was one of them that sat at the table with him.

3 Then took Mary a pound of ointment of spikenard, very costly, and anointed the feet of Jesus, and wiped his feet with her hair: and the house was filled with the odour of the ointment.

4 Then saith one of his disciples, Judas Iscariot, Simon's son, which should betray him,

5 Why was not this ointment sold for three hundred pence, and given to the poor?

6 This he said, not that he cared for the poor; but because he was a thief, and had the bag, and bare what was put therein.

7 Then said Jesus, Let her alone: against the day of my burying hath she kept this.

8 For the poor always ye have with you; but me ye have not always.

■ THE LESSON EXPLAINED

Setting Priorities (Luke 10:38–42)

Guests for dinner. All hands on deck! Check off the work to be done: table set, food prepared, foot-washing basin in place. What have I forgotten?

Mary, what are you doing? Why are you sitting down on the job? Get up here and help! Jesus, You know how busy I am, how much work it takes to get dinner ready. Tell my sister to get up and help me.

Now, Martha, calm down. Think for a minute. Why all the fuss and bother? Can't we eat a simple meal together? Mary is interested in learning about the Father's kingdom. Do you have no time to listen? No excuses, Martha. Our world may not think women have the right or need to listen to religious teaching. I want everyone, male and female, young and old, to listen. Only by hearing the Word can you enter the kingdom.

Showing Love (John 12:1–3)

Martha must have been a great cook. She worked hard at it, and Jesus kept coming back for her meals. She certainly had reason to do something for Jesus. He had taken her dead brother and given him back alive. What an extra effort she must have put in to make this supper special for Jesus.

Mary had another way of thanking Jesus: an expensive gift. She either took her own prized possession or spent a large sum of money for perfume imported from India. Bowing before Jesus like the lowest servant, she poured the perfume on His feet and then used her hair like a towel to wipe away the excess and wash His feet. The strong, sweet perfume filled the house.

Searching Out Motives (John 12:4–8)

Wasteful. Horribly wasteful. Why spend a year's wages on an act so quickly finished with no lasting results? The poor can use the money a lot better, and we always give gifts to the poor at Passover. Tell her how wrong she is. So responded Judas Iscariot, who was becoming somewhat of an expert on wrong himself. As treasurer for the disciples, he would receive the money and be responsible for giving it to the poor. He knew a poor person who needed it.

Jesus showed a higher motive for giving. Helping the poor might be just a holiday habit. Preparing Jesus symbolically for death was a one-time action history would never forget. Helping the poor is a habit never to be forgotten or ignored. Finding a unique way to serve Jesus calls for impulsive, sacrificial action by a person open to what God is working in the world.

TRUTHS TO LIVE BY

People serve Jesus in different ways. Martha planned, cooked, served, and hosted. Mary impulsively acted as the occasion demanded. Both served Jesus, but Mary gained greater praise. She did what the situation demanded, not what habit and custom dictated.

Proper service pleases Jesus, not people. Too often acts of service follow habit and please people's needs to be comfortable. Serving Jesus requires you to forget human opinions and seek Jesus' opinion.

Proper service fits proper action to immediate moment. People want rules that show you what to do and when to do it. Jesus said to pay attention to what is most needed to show what God is doing now. Listening to God's Word may be more important than action. Participating in a work God is doing may be more important than feeding poor people right now.

VERSES TO REMEMBER

And Jesus answered and said unto her, Martha, Martha, thou art careful and troubled about many things: But one thing is needful: and Mary hath chosen that good part, which shall not be taken away from her.—Luke 10:41–42

DAILY BIBLE READINGS

Jan. 6 — Mary and Martha Send for Jesus. John 11:1–15
Jan. 7 — Martha Believed in the Resurrection. John 11:17–27
Jan. 8 — Mary Believed in Jesus' Power. John 11:28–36
Jan. 9 — Jesus Raised Lazarus from the Dead. John 11:38–44
Jan. 10 — Jesus Anointed by Mary of Bethany. Mark 14:3–9
Jan. 11 — Women Minister to Jesus' Body. Matt. 27:51–56
Jan. 12 — Be Confident in the Lord. Ps. 27:1–6

Peter

Matthew 4:18–20; 16:13–23

The cherub face of the twenty-five-year-old man lingers forever in my memory. A summer spent working at a Christian resort center led him to Christ. Wanting to learn more, he applied for admission to the seminary. Faculty dilemma: do you admit someone to a seminary who has no training or membership in a local church? The young man's personal enthusiasm convinced the faculty to make one major exception to admission rules. Soon the local church had the privilege of baptizing a seminary student, then performing his marriage ceremony, then ordaining him to ministry. When he heard Jesus say, Follow me, he acted just like Peter. He left everything—family, occupation, school—to follow.

■ THE BIBLE LESSON

18 And Jesus, walking by the sea of Galilee, saw two brethren, Simon called Peter, and Andrew his brother, casting a net into the sea: for they were fishers.

19 And he saith unto them, Follow me, and I will make you fishers of men.

20 And they straightway left their nets, and followed him.

. . . .

13 When Jesus came into the coasts of Caesarea Philippi, he asked his disciples, saying, Whom do men say that I the Son of man am?

14 And they said, Some say that thou art John the Baptist: some, Elias; and others, Jeremias, or one of the prophets.

15 He saith unto them, But whom say ye that I am?

16 And Simon Peter answered and said, Thou art the Christ, the Son of the living God.

17 And Jesus answered and said unto him, Blessed art thou, Simon Barjona: for flesh and blood hath not revealed it unto thee, but my Father which is in heaven.

18 And I say also unto thee, That thou art Peter, and upon this rock I will build my church; and the gates of hell shall not prevail against it.

19 And I will give unto thee the keys of the kingdom of heaven: and whatsoever thou shalt bind on earth shall be bound in heaven: and whatsoever thou shalt loose on earth shall be loosed in heaven.

20 Then charged he his disciples that they should tell no man that he was Jesus the Christ.

21 From that time forth began Jesus to shew unto his disciples, how that he must go unto Jerusalem, and suffer many things of the elders and chief priests and scribes, and be killed, and be raised again the third day.

22 Then Peter took him, and began to rebuke him, saying, Be it far from thee, Lord: this shall not be unto thee.

23 But he turned, and said unto Peter, Get thee behind me, Satan: thou art an offence unto me: for thou savourest not the things that be of God, but those that be of men.

■ THE LESSON EXPLAINED

Decision to Follow (4:18–20)

No miracles. No crowds. No disciples. Just a baptism scene and the temptations story. Then a lone preacher walks by the beautiful sea saying the kingdom of God is present in Him so people should repent. How do you respond to Him? Two professional fishermen took their muscled, tanned bodies away from the fishing boats and nets. They gave up their profession and family to follow the preacher. He gave them a new career: fishing for people. How foolish, said the world. You are the first fruits of God's eternal kingdom, said Jesus. Who was right?

Question to Answer (16:13–15)

Many months, miles, and miracles pass. Crowds mob Jesus. Religious people ridicule Him and want to kill Him. Time for a showdown. What have the disciples learned in these months? Do they understand anything? They have been listening to the crowds. They know the common people's opinions: Jesus is a great prophet returned to earth, probably preparing for Messiah's coming. Knowing popular opinion is not enough, Jesus pressed the question deeper: You—yes, you—whom do you think I am? You must give a personal answer to this most important of all questions.

Confession to Make (16:16–20)

The first convert has become the speaker for the disciples. Following his compulsive nature, Peter blurts out an answer: You are the Messiah, the Son of the living God. Holy insight, that's what you have, replies Jesus. Human reasoning would never come to that opinion. No one but God Himself could lead you to such a confession. The confession means you have a mission. You have explained who I am. I will explain who you are. You are named Peter, a word that means rock. Well, Rock, I will build My church on you. Yes, a group of followers will gather around you to worship Me, the King of the new kingdom. You all will be in deadly battle against the powers of hell. You will win. The church will prevail. Peter, as representative of the church you will lead the church in witnessing, preaching, ministering. This will lead still others to join the worshiping community of believers, all of whom will have the keys to bind and loose, that is to witness to Christ, making entrance to the kingdom available (see Matt. 18:18). But Peter, that is for the future. For the present you must keep this confession silent and learn more about your mission.

Lifestyle to Adopt (16:21–23)

Peter, you and the church will have the keys to the kingdom, but this means you will also suffer the perils of the kingdom. I am on the road to Jerusalem. Religious leaders out to get Me will succeed. They will kill Me. But I will be raised on the third day.

Kill You? Did I hear You say, they will kill You? Forget it, Lord. No one can kill You. You are the King. You will establish the kingdom. We will have the keys to the kingdom and share Your power. Don't ever talk about such things anymore. You cannot die. You must not die. Then the kingdom would die.

Rock, you have changed character. You have become Satan. The powers of Hell are prevailing in your life now. Get away from Me. You have quit listening to God's voice. Now you are using human reasoning. You have so much to learn before you and the church can admit people to the kingdom. You must find the suffering lifestyle of kingdom people.

■ TRUTHS TO LIVE BY

God calls you to follow Him immediately. Accepting God's call means changing your life now. You do not simply add a little bit new to your life. You let God absolutely change your priorities, your use of time, your conduct at home and work. You become a rock who lives God's lifestyle and whom God uses to witness and minister so that still other people can enter His kingdom.

God calls you to know who Jesus is. Jesus is the Messiah, the Son of God. He fulfills all the hopes and promises of the Bible. He is also the One who suffered and died. The only path to hope and promise is through the Cross. You must be ready to die for Christ if you expect to be part of His kingdom.

God calls you to keep on learning. Satan keeps fighting for you. He wants to control your life just because you say Christ does. Satan easily slips into your ears nice-sounding words that let you defend and protect God. God wants you to have more than one experience with Him. He wants to reveal truth to you every day so that Satan cannot deceive you.

■ A VERSE TO REMEMBER

And Simon Peter answered and said, Thou art the Christ, the Son of the living God.—Matthew 16:16

■ DAILY BIBLE READINGS

Jan. 13 — The Calling of Simon Peter. Mark 1:14–20
Jan. 14 — Peter's Pentecost Sermon. Acts 2:14–20
Jan. 15 — Peter Confirms Jesus' Resurrection. Acts 2:22–36
Jan. 16 — Peter Raised Two Persons from the Dead. Acts 9:32–42
Jan. 17 — Peter's Vision of Food. Acts 10:9–16
Jan. 18 — Peter Visits Cornelius. Acts 10:17–23
Jan. 19 — Peter's Sermon to Cornelius. Acts 10:34–43

Judas Iscariot

Matthew 26:14–16, 20–25, 47–50; 27:1–5

Judas! Dare one find an illustration to compare with Judas? The name itself illustrates the darkest side of humanity. You and I can each pick out some incident in our life when we let somebody down. We told a lie to parents to get to do something. We tried to fool a teacher about a homework assignment. We tried to hide a business failing from the boss. Or we can point to an Aaron Burr or a CIA double agent who betrayed our country. Nothing we point to, however, brings up emotional feeling to compare with the one word—Judas. Why?

■ THE BIBLE LESSON

14 Then one of the twelve, called Judas Iscariot, went unto the chief priests,

15 And said unto them, What will ye give me, and I will deliver him unto you? And they covenanted with him for thirty pieces of silver.

16 And from that time he sought opportunity to betray him.

....

20 Now when the even was come, he sat down with the twelve.

21 And as they did eat, he said, Verily I say unto you, that one of you shall betray me.

22 And they were exceeding sorrowful, and began every one of them to say unto him, Lord, is it I?

23 And he answered and said, He that dippeth his hand with me in the dish, the same shall betray me.

24 The Son of man goeth as it is written of him: but woe unto that man by whom the Son of man is betrayed! it had been good for that man if he had not been born.

25 Then Judas, which betrayed him, answered and said, Master, is it I? He said unto him, Thou hast said.

47 And while he yet spake, lo, Judas, one of the twelve, came, and with him a great multitude with swords and staves, from the chief priests and elders of the people.

48 Now he that betrayed him gave them a sign, saying, Whomsoever I shall kiss, that same is he: hold him fast.

49 And forthwith he came to Jesus, and said, Hail, master; and kissed him.

50 And Jesus said unto him, Friend, wherefore art thou come? Then came they, and laid hands on Jesus, and took him.

. . . .

1 When the morning was come, all the chief priests and elders of the people took counsel against Jesus to put him to death:

2 And when they had bound him, they led him away, and delivered him to Pontius Pilate the governor.

3 Then Judas, which had betrayed him, when he saw that he was condemned, repented himself, and brought again the thirty pieces of silver to the chief priests and elders,

4 Saying, I have sinned in that I have betrayed the innocent blood. And they said, What is that to us? see thou to that.

5 And he cast down the pieces of silver in the temple, and departed, and went and hanged himself.

THE LESSON EXPLAINED

The Traitor Commissioned (26:14–16)

He is determined to go through with it. He is going to let them kill Him. The dream is gone. No kingdom. No freedom from Rome. No power, glory, and riches for us who have trudged the roads of Galilee these many months with Him. Well, I might as well get out of it what I can. The priests want to kill Him. What is it worth to them? I will go and see. Thirty pieces of silver! A person would have to work three months to make that much money. At least I'll get something for all this wasted time. Now to find the right time and place.

The Traitor Identified (26:20–25)

Passover! The glory days of our nation. We showed the strongest nation on earth that our God could destroy them any time He wanted to. Why doesn't He do it again this Passover, just destroy the Roman armies and free us to be His nation again, let Jesus truly become king? That's what He promised. What is Jesus saying? He knows one of us will betray Him. How can He know? Have the priests betrayed me? Why, look. All the others think they might be guilty. They suspect nothing. What? Jesus pronounced a woe on the betrayer. I should be afraid, but He has not delivered on promises of kingship. He can't deliver on this either. Guess I better join with the others and ask. "Is it I, Teacher?"

"You said it." What did He mean by that? He seems to know what I am to do, but He does not accuse me publicly. He just whispers and lets me make the choice. I said it, but I do not have to do it.

The Traitor in Action (26:47–50)

The time is right. He did what He always does in tense moments. He ducked away to His private place to pray. No one will see us. Come on, let's go for it. I have sure planned it well: a kiss to identify Him. Others will think I am showing my affection and care in this desperate moment. What, He still calls me, "Friend." What does He mean? Is He asking me what I am up to? (KJV) Or is He telling me to get on with it? (NASB) It's out of my hands. The priests will do their work, now.

The Traitor in Despair (27:1–5)

It is done. The Romans have Him. What have I done? He does not deserve to die. He is a good man. He was a friend. He loved me. Stop this! Priests, take your money back. Stop this trial. He is innocent. . . .They will not do anything. They are going to let Him die. It's my fault. Take your money. It will do me no good now. I have no reason to live. I killed the

One who loved me most. Here's the noose. Around the tree. On my neck. Now jump. AAAAHHHH!

■ TRUTHS TO LIVE BY

Loving money is evil's root. The disciples knew Judas's interest in money. They chose him to be treasurer. They did not know an interest had become an obsession. Judas dared steal the little that Jesus and His disciples had to live on. This started him on the road to betrayal. He loved money more than he loved Jesus. And you?

Loving money makes people expendable. For three months' normal wages, Judas betrayed the best person he ever knew. He valued money more than friendship and life. He would never put that in words. He put it in action. And you?

Loving money leads to irreversible actions. Jesus gave Judas chances to change. Judas refused. Only when the course of action could not be stopped did he see the error of his ways. Guilt and sorrow poured over him to the point of despair. Suicide! You still have a chance to choose Jesus over money. Will you?

■ A VERSE TO REMEMBER

Then Judas, which betrayed him, answered and said, Master, is it I? He said unto him, Thou hast said.—Matthew 26:25

■ DAILY BIBLE READINGS

Jan. 20 — Judas Named One of the Disciples. Matt. 10:1–6
Jan. 21 — Jesus Knew Who Would Betray Him. John 6:60–65
Jan. 22 — One Disciple Acknowledged to Be Devil. John 6:66–71
Jan. 23 — Judas Contacted the Chief Priests. Luke 22:1–6
Jan. 24 — Jesus Dismisses Judas from Supper. John 13:21–30
Jan. 25 — Jesus' Betrayal and Arrest. Luke 22:47–53
Jan. 26 — Judas's Replacement. Acts 1:15–26

Barnabas

Acts 4:32–37; 9:26–27; 11:22–30

Marvin has many claims to fame. Decades of teaching have produced friends and colleagues all over the world. A strong publishing career has let the world see the brilliance and incisiveness of his mind. Close friends know him as a dedicated family man who sacrificed much for his wife and children. I know him in a unique way. He taught me in only one class. I left the school not sure he knew my name. Six years later a job offer came my way. Marvin had recommended me for the position. Why? Because Marvin was loyal to his students, knew us even better than we thought, and gave encouragement at every step of the way. Decades have passed. I have come to know Marvin as a friend and colleague who has contributed much to my life as scholar and as person. I will ever remember him, however, as encourager. Marvin was my Barnabas.

■ THE BIBLE LESSON

32 And the multitude of them that believed were of one heart and of one soul: neither said any of them that ought of the things which he possessed was his own; but they had all things common.

....

36 And Joses, who by the apostles was surnamed Barnabas, (which is, being interpreted, The son of consolation,) a Levite, and of the country of Cyprus,

37 Having land, sold it, and brought the money, and laid it at the apostles' feet.

....

26 And when Saul was come to Jerusalem, he assayed to join himself to the disciples: but they were all afraid of him, and believed not that he was a disciple.

27 But Barnabas took him, and brought him to the apostles, and declared unto them how he had seen the Lord in the way, and that he had spoken to him, and how he had preached boldly at Damascus in the name of Jesus.

....

22 Then tidings of these things came unto the ears of the church which was in Jerusalem: and they sent forth Barnabas, that he should go as far as Antioch.

23 Who, when he came, and had seen the grace of God, was glad, and exhorted them all, that with purpose of heart they would cleave unto the Lord.

24 For he was a good man, and full of the Holy Ghost and of faith: and much people was added unto the Lord.

25 Then departed Barnabas to Tarsus, for to seek Saul:

26 And when he had found him, he brought him unto Antioch. And it came to pass, that a whole year they assembled themselves with the church, and taught much people. And the disciples were called Christians first in Antioch.

27 And in these days came prophets from Jerusalem unto Antioch.

28 And there stood up one of them named Agabus, and signified by the spirit that there should be great dearth throughout all the world: which came to pass in the days of Claudius Caesar.

29 Then the disciples, every man according to his ability, determined to send relief unto the brethren which dwelt in Judaea:

30 Which also they did, and sent it to the elders by the hands of Barnabas and Saul.

■ THE LESSON EXPLAINED

Encourager with Possessions (4:32–37)

Koinonia marked the early church. The Greek word is difficult to translate: fellowship, community, generosity, sharing, unity, intimate relationship. The Jerusalem church outwardly expressed this closeness as each member placed personal possessions in the hands of the entire fellowship of believers. Such fellowship empowered the leadership to preach the gospel. The Holy Spirit inspired Luke to set out one major example of this. Joses was a foreigner, a Jewish priest who grew up in Cyprus but lived in Jerusalem. He sold the land that he owned, took the money, and gave it to the apostles to help the church. This example and his personal life led the fellowship to give this fellow a new name: Barnabas, the one who consoles or encourages.

Encourager of the Underdog (9:23–32)

The fellowship suffered. Their nemesis: one man named Saul of Tarsus. He went house to house finding believers and leading them to prison and even to death. Dare anyone name the name of Jesus or admit to belonging to the fellowship? God took care of that. He overwhelmed Saul and made him a believer. Another fellowship crisis. Would anyone believe Saul's conversion? Was this not another trick to discover more believers for prison? Barnabas stood up. He encouraged the young convert and encouraged the disciples to accept him as one of them. Now Saul faced the danger he had enforced.

Encourager of the Underprivileged (11:19–30)

Persecution of the fellowship continued. Stephen was stoned, the first Christian martyr. The church expanded, leaving Jerusalem to preach to Jews everywhere. Some from roots similar to those of Barnabas went further. They preached to Gentiles, with success. Jerusalem had to know about such radical mission strategy. How would they react? They chose the trusted encourager Barnabas to examine the situation. Why? "Barnabas was a 'bridge-builder' able to see the positive aspects in both sides of an issue and to mediate between perspectives" (J. Polhill, *Acts*, NAC 26, 272). Off to Antioch to investigate. Findings: God's grace evidently at work. Result: Accept the foreigners, encouraging them to obey God faithfully and enthusiastically. Revival broke out again. How come? An encourager let God's Spirit lead him through the fellowship's crisis of faith to victory. Then seeing the situation was more than he could handle, he found one with the gifts to work in the situation: Paul. Things did not always go smoothly. God indicated famine was on the way. The Antioch fellowship responded. They sent Barnabas and Saul back to Jerusalem with encouragement: relief aid.

■ TRUTHS TO LIVE BY

Fellowship distinguishes the church from the world. People in your town see you and your church either as people fussing and fighting like they do or as people with a different spirit helping one another in unusual ways. How do they see you?

Encouragement helps, but doubt destroys fellowship. New days bring new crises of belief for the church. Can God truly be working among known sinners and enemies of the church, among rich who bring gifts to the church, among foreigners who preach where the church has feared to go, in disaster situations? Do you encourage "strange" works of God, or discourage them with doubt?

Fellowship is fostered by a few good people. Barnabas knew his limits. He sought help when he had to, but he did what he could. He earned the church's respect because he encouraged, because he obeyed the Holy Spirit, and because he was good. Anyone can do that. Do you?

■ VERSES TO REMEMBER

Who, when he came, and had seen the grace of God, was glad, and exhorted them all, that with purpose of heart they would cleave unto the Lord. For he was a good man, and full of the Holy Ghost and of faith: and much people was added unto the Lord.—Acts 11:23–24

■ DAILY BIBLE READINGS

Jan. 27 — Barnabas and Paul Called to Ministry.
　　　　　Acts 13:1–5
Jan. 28 — Barnabas and Paul Minister in Iconium.
　　　　　Acts 14:1–7
Jan. 29 — Barnabas and Paul Minister in Lystra.
　　　　　Acts 14:11–18
Jan. 30 — Barnabas and Paul Sent to Jerusalem.
　　　　　Acts 15:1–11
Jan. 31 — Barnabas and Paul Sent to Antioch. Acts 15:22–29
Feb.　1 — Barnabas and Paul Separate. Acts 15:36–41
Feb.　2 — Barnabas and Paul Reunited. Gal. 2:1–10

Stephen

Acts 6:1–8:3

Zig! As boys we all wanted to visit Zig. The fascinating stories made us want to look at him. We really wanted to see his back or his legs. He had suffered in a prisoner of war camp. His diet there became more legendary each time the story was repeated. Someone who suffered so for the country, we wanted a look at. Zig had one advantage on Stephen. He lived. Stephen died, not for his country but for his faith. Do you think Stephen would have thought Zig had an advantage?

◼ THE BIBLE LESSON

8 And Stephen, full of faith and power, did great wonders and miracles among the people.

9 Then there arose certain of the synagogue, which is called the synagogue of the Libertines, and Cyrenians, and Alexandrians, and of them of Cilicia and of Asia, disputing with Stephen.

10 And they were not able to resist the wisdom and the spirit by which he spake.

11 Then they suborned men, which said, We have heard him speak blasphemous words against Moses, and against God.

12 And they stirred up the people, and the elders, and the scribes, and came upon him, and caught him, and brought him to the council,

13 And set up false witnesses, which said, This man ceaseth not to speak blasphemous words against this holy place, and the law:

14 For we have heard him say, that this Jesus of Nazareth shall destroy this place, and shall change the customs which Moses delivered us.

15 And all that sat in the council, looking stedfastly on him, saw his face as it had been the face of an angel.

....

54 When they heard these things, they were cut to the heart, and they gnashed on him with their teeth.

55 But he, being full of the Holy Ghost, looked up stedfastly into heaven, and saw the glory of God, and Jesus standing on the right hand of God,

56 And said, Behold, I see the heavens opened, and the Son of man standing on the right hand of God.

57 Then they cried out with a loud voice, and stopped their ears, and ran upon him with one accord,

58 And cast him out of the city, and stoned him: and the witnesses laid down their clothes at a young man's feet, whose name was Saul.

59 And they stoned Stephen, calling upon God, and saying, Lord Jesus, receive my spirit.

60 And he kneeled down, and cried with a loud voice, Lord, lay not this sin to their charge. And when he had said this, he fell asleep.

■ THE LESSON EXPLAINED

The Deacon's Service (6:1–10)

Problems in the church. Fellowship broken, racism rising. Aramaic-speaking members neglect the welfare needs of the Greek-speaking believers. Now the disciples have to delay their ministry of preaching the gospel to settle fights in the church. Must be a better way. Elect a group to take care of church administration and problems. Let the preachers preach. The new officials must be highly qualified: honest, respected, wise, good administrators, and above all full of God's Holy Spirit. Heading the list: Stephen, a person of faith and of the Spirit. What do you know? Solve the problems, and the church grows again. Even some Jewish priests came to believe on Christ.

Stephen went beyond expectations, becoming the first person besides the apostles to do miracles. Ironically, Stephen met problems from people he should have included as his own: Greek-speaking Jews who had moved to Jerusalem from foreign countries. Their zeal for Judaism made them fight the gospel harder than anyone else. They framed a charge against Stephen.

The Deacon's Summons and Sermon (6:11–7:53)

The frame worked. Not only religious leaders but even the common people believed Stephen was a blasphemer. The charge was much like that against Jesus. As was His, the trial was a mockery of justice. Even when God gave Stephen a holy glow, the priests and people did not flinch. They wanted blood. They did give Stephen a chance to testify. He gave the longest sermon in the New Testament. He repeated the history of Israel, especially Abraham and Moses up to David and Solomon. That holy history saw God's goodness and Israel's resistance and rebellion. That history climaxed when God sent His "Just One" whom the priests and people betrayed and killed. The lovers of the law are not keepers of the law.

The Deacon's Stoning (7:54–60)

What response do you expect to such a sermon? God responded to Stephen with a vision of the ascended Christ and the glory of God. That angered the mob further. They protected their law by not doing anything so violent in the holy city. Once outside the city, they let loose their fury. They stoned Stephen to death. To do so, they took off their outer garments to get freedom to throw stones. Saul of Tarsus got to protect the garments. He also got to hear Stephen pray: receive my spirit, but do not count them guilty for what they do. The deacon died.

■ TRUTHS TO LIVE BY

Deacons Dismantle Dissension. Churches find reasons to disagree, even fight. God uses deacons as His servant leaders to bring peace. Deacons never have reason to lead one part of a church against another. God calls deacons to resolve conflicts.

Deacons Dispute Detractors. Deacons know God's history with His people and testify to it when others deny it. Deacons see what people are true to God's dealings with His people and what people deny their heritage. Peacemakers in the church, deacons often find themselves in the midst of fire outside the church.

Deacons Die before Denying. Deacons remain true to God's calling in Christ no matter who opposes them and no matter what price they must pay. Christ is worth their life. Christ is worth dying for. Deacons follow Stephen's example, praying for those who oppose and even kill them.

A VERSE TO REMEMBER

And Stephen, full of faith and power, did great wonders and miracles among the people.—Acts 6:8

DAILY BIBLE READINGS

Feb. 3	—	Stephen Chosen to Be Deacon. Acts 6:1–7
Feb. 4	—	Stephen's Testimony Before High Priest. Acts 7:1–10
Feb. 5	—	Stiff-Necked People Resist the Holy Spirit. Acts 7:44–53
Feb. 6	—	Gain True Life by Enduring Persecution. Luke 21:10–19
Feb. 7	—	Take Refuge in God. Ps. 57:1–11
Feb. 8	—	Pray for Those Who Persecute You. Matthew 5:43–46
Feb. 9	—	Acknowledge God Before People. Luke 12:4–12

Priscilla and Aquila

Acts 18:1–4, 18–19, 24–26; Romans 16:3–5

The early morning phone jangled me awake. No! Cannot believe it. Gwynn and Garth are not coming from England to visit us today. Gwynn just found Garth dead in his bed, plane tickets on the bedside table. One of life's saddest memories. Yet Gwynn and Garth also provided some of life's brightest memories. The two Welsh lovelies (to use their word for others) demonstrated to us year after year in their church in Billericay, England, what it meant to serve God as devoted parents, Bible teachers, deacon, and youth group leaders. The church hardly needed a pastor, only a preacher. Gwynn and Garth led out in most of the rest of the work. They continued the tradition of Priscilla and Aquila.

■ THE BIBLE LESSON

ACTS 18

1 After these things Paul departed from Athens, and came to Corinth;

2 And found a certain Jew named Aquila, born in Pontus, lately come from Italy, with his wife Priscilla; (because that Claudius had commanded all Jews to depart from Rome:) and came unto them.

3 And because he was of the same craft, he abode with them, and wrought: for by their occupation they were tentmakers.

4 And he reasoned in the synagogue every sabbath, and persuaded the Jews and the Greeks.

. . . .

18 And Paul after this tarried there yet a good while, and then took his leave of the brethren, and sailed thence into Syria, and with him Priscilla and Aquila; having shorn his head in Cenchrea: for he had a vow.

19 And he came to Ephesus, and left them there: but he himself entered into the synagogue, and reasoned with the Jews.

. . . .

24 And a certain Jew named Apollos, born at Alexandria, an eloquent man, and mighty in the scriptures, came to Ephesus.

25 This man was instructed in the way of the Lord; and being fervent in the spirit, he spake and taught diligently the things of the Lord, knowing only the baptism of John.

26 And he began to speak boldly in the synagogue: whom when Aquila and Priscilla had heard, they took him unto them, and expounded unto him the way of God more perfectly.

. . . .

ROMANS 16

3 Greet Priscilla and Aquila my helpers in Christ Jesus:

4 Who have for my life laid down their own necks: unto whom not only I give thanks, but also all the churches of the Gentiles.

5 Likewise greet the church that is in their house.

THE LESSON EXPLAINED

Suffering Together for Christ (Acts 18:1–4)

New city. New synagogue. New persecution. New ministry to Gentiles. So went Paul's life as he followed God's missionary call. Then came Corinth, the largest, most cosmopolitan, most Roman, and most immoral city of Greece. Here Aquila and Priscilla (Luke's popular name for the woman Paul addresses more formally as Prisca in Rom. 16:3; 1 Cor. 16:19; 2 Tim. 4:19) entered Paul's life. They could play one-up with Paul. The Roman emperor Claudius had driven them from Rome in A.D. 49 because they were Christian leaders. Now they, like Paul, had no permanent home. They traveled for Christ. Like Paul, as tentmakers or leather workers, they could set up shop and work wherever they traveled. In

Corinth, persecution experiences, Christian commitment, and common occupation bound the couple to Paul.

Traveling Together for Christ (Acts 18:18-19)

God had a special interest in Corinth and let Paul remain there over eighteen months, longer than any place he had yet visited (vv. 9-11,18). Priscilla and Aquila ministered with him. When God led Paul to leave, Priscilla and Aquila closed their shop and traveled with him to Ephesus, where Paul ministered briefly. When he left, they stayed, preparing the way for his return for a three-year ministry there (19:10, 22; 20:31).

Discipling Together for Christ (Acts 18:24-26)

Paul had no monopoly on missionary ministry. A highly-skilled Jew from Alexandria, Egypt, also came to Ephesus. Few could match his preaching skills, certainly not Paul. This man knew the Hebrew Scriptures and preached them powerfully. Though Luke's description is open to several interpretations, he apparently pictures Apollos "as a Christian" who "knew the way of the Lord, taught accurately about Jesus, and *may* have experienced the Spirit" (Polhill, *Acts*, NAC 26, 396). He lacked one thing. John the Baptist baptized him. He did not understand Christian baptism. Ephesus, as a beginning church, had no pastor to teach him. Faithful Aquila and Priscilla took on the task. A skilled, zealous laborer for Christ matured and gained ministry skills because concerned laypeople cared enough and had courage enough both to confront and to instruct him.

Sacrificing Together for Christ (Rom. 16:3-5)

Six or seven years have passed. Emperor Claudius has died. Aquila and Priscilla have returned to Rome. Paul writes to introduce himself, his theology, and his ministry to the church at Rome. He concludes by renewing his ministerial network with greetings. Priscilla and Aquila head the list. They have shared the work God gave Paul. They risked their necks for him, possibly using social, financial, or political influence. They had such influence as business people able to travel and build homes in different cities. They used teaching skills and financial resources to help Gentile churches. In Rome they opened their home to the church as its meeting place. Possessions and social class did not control them. They used and sacrificed all they had for Christ.

■ TRUTHS TO LIVE BY

God uses the laity. Laypeople often turn the church over to professional staff, who are tempted to exercise strong pastoral authority. God still looks for people like Priscilla and Aquila who use their business career as a means to serve God.

God works through life's "tragedies." Being run out of Rome could have been the end of the world for Priscilla and Aquila. Instead, it became the beginning of missionary service.

God uses lay people to teach preachers. Paul and Apollos enhanced their ministry skills and work because Priscilla and Aquila cared for them and showed them how to improve, even risking their lives for one preacher.

■ VERSES TO REMEMBER

Greet Priscilla and Aquila my helpers in Christ Jesus: Who have for my life laid down their own necks: unto whom not only I give thanks, but also all the churches of the Gentiles.
—Romans 16:3–4

■ DAILY BIBLE READINGS

Feb. 10 — They Acknowledged Other Churches. 1 Cor. 16:15–24
Feb. 11 — They Supported Paul's Teachings. Acts 18:5–11
Feb. 12 — Each Person Has a Special Duty. 1 Cor. 3:5–11
Feb. 13 — Support Others' Work. Rom. 12:1–8
Feb. 14 — Share Christian Lifestyles. Rom. 12:9–14
Feb. 15 — Fulfill the Law of Love. Rom. 13:8–14
Feb. 16 — Respect Your Leaders. 1 Thess. 5:12–22

Timothy

Acts 16:1–5; 1 Corinthians 4:14–17; Philippians 2:19–22; 2 Timothy 1:4–7

Asbjorn made me proud. Now heaven is proud to claim him as one of theirs. As I diligently worked on my first publication projects as a young professor, Asbjorn took his role as student assistant seriously. He found every article I needed, summarized it, and indicated how it might help what I was writing. He critiqued the sentences I wrote. He left for home in Norway. I returned to the States. We followed one another in the newspapers. Following Asbjorn was not hard. He became a world leader in youth ministry. Only eternity can name the multitude of lives changed because he steadfastly worked for his Lord. In some minor way Asbjorn was a Timothy whom my ministry sent into the Lord's harvest.

■ THE BIBLE LESSON

ACTS 16

1 Then came he to Derbe and Lystra: and, behold, a certain disciple was there, named Timotheus, the son of a certain woman, which was a Jewess, and believed; but his father was a Greek:

2 Which was well reported of by the brethren that were at Lystra and Iconium.

3 Him would Paul have to go forth with him; and took and circumcised him because of the Jews which were in those quarters: for they knew all that his father was a Greek.

4 And as they went through the cities, they delivered them the decrees for to keep, that were ordained of the apostles and elders which were at Jerusalem.

5 And so were the churches established in the faith, and increased in number daily.

1 CORINTHIANS 4

14 I write not these things to shame you, but as my beloved sons I warn you.

15 For though ye have ten thousand instructors in Christ, yet have ye not many fathers: for in Christ Jesus I have begotten you through the gospel.

16 Wherefore I beseech you, be ye followers of me.

17 For this cause have I sent unto you Timotheus, who is my beloved son, and faithful in the Lord, who shall bring you into remembrance of my ways which be in Christ, as I teach every where in every church.

PHILIPPIANS 2

19 But I trust in the Lord Jesus to send Timotheus shortly unto you, that I also may be of good comfort, when I know your state.

20 For I have no man like-minded, who will naturally care for your state.

21 For all seek their own, not the things which are Jesus Christ's.

22 But ye know the proof of him, that, as a son with the father, he hath served with me in the gospel.

2 TIMOTHY 1

4 Greatly desiring to see thee, being mindful of thy tears, that I may be filled with joy;

5 When I call to remembrance the unfeigned faith that is in thee, which dwelt first in thy grandmother Lois, and thy mother Eunice; and I am persuaded that in thee also.

6 Wherefore I put thee in remembrance that thou stir up the gift of God, which is in thee by the putting on of my hands.

7 For God hath not given us the spirit of fear; but of power, and of love, and of a sound mind.

THE LESSON EXPLAINED

Prepared for Service (Acts 16:1–5)

Pleasant surprise: To return to a place of ministry and find a young man matured and ready to join you in ministry. Timothy stood ready when Paul returned to Lystra, the small military outpost in the south-central part of modern Turkey. One problem: Was Timothy Jew or Greek? Jewish mother provided religious training, but Greek father apparently prevented circumcision as a baby. Jews would accept his religion but not his person. Greeks would accept his person but not his religion. He lived without clear racial identity in a society proud of such identity. Still, he ministered. Churches twenty miles away in Iconium testified to that. Wanting a partner in ministry able to speak to Jews and Greeks, Paul gave Timothy what he lacked, circumcising him and making his identity clear. Now he could minister with no questions asked. His ministry quickly bore fruit.

Trusted for Service (1 Cor. 4:14–17)

How can I make you hear me? So Paul cried out to the Corinthians, a church with divided loyalties. Apparently they used each new word from a different preacher to start their fighting all over again (see 1:12). Paul loved them. He had started the church (Acts 18). He was their father in the faith. He wanted them to stay true to the teachings and lifestyle he had taught them. His words and writing did not seem to work. New approach: send Timothy. What a task for a young minister: accomplish what his father in the faith could not. How much trust Paul placed in Timothy!

Caring in Service (Phil. 2:19–22)

Different situations call for different ministries. Corinth needed warning and teaching. Philippi needed loving care and comfort. Timothy was the minister for both situations. Why? Because he could be trusted to determine the truth of a situation. He was like-minded (literally, "like-souled") with Paul, committed totally to the ones to whom they ministered instead of to themselves. The cause of Jesus dominated all he did. Both Paul and the church knew his reputation through personal experience. He served the gospel well.

Gifted for Service (2 Tim. 1:4–7)

The end nears for the aged apostle. How does he want to face the end? With Timothy! The one he prayed for every day. The one he had cried with in a tense moment of ministry. The one whose presence brought joy to his life. The one with genuine faith taught from his childhood by devoted mother and grandmother. The one using spiritual gifts so splendidly and needing to move to an even more mature use of those gifts as his mentor, friend, and father in the faith passed on. He needed to remember his ordination in which Paul laid hands on him and use that as motivation to grow in ministry skills and commitment. Youth was no longer an excuse for fear and timidity. Timothy had to show love, self-discipline, and power in his ministry. God gave the gifts. It was time for Timothy to use them fully.

■ TRUTHS TO LIVE BY

Ministry is not a solo performance. Paul fathered Timothy in the ministry. The time came for Timothy to strengthen and encourage Paul. Ministers need to be soul mates helping each other, not soloists envious or fearful of one another.

Ministry requires spiritual growth. One never becomes an expert in ministry. Ministry is always a new day with God with new challenges to discover, train, and rededicate the spiritual gifts He gives. What gifts has He given you? Are you actively using and stirring them up for His service?

Ministry gives and receives encouragement. Paul constantly encouraged Timothy and sent Timothy out to encourage others. Who receives hope and courage in ministry through you. Whom do you depend on for hope and courage?

■ A VERSE TO REMEMBER

For this cause have I sent unto you Timotheus, who is my beloved son, and faithful in the Lord, who shall bring you into remembrance of my ways which be in Christ, as I teach every where in every church.—1 Corinthians 4:17

■ DAILY BIBLE READINGS

Feb. 17 — Timothy Worked in Corinth. 1 Cor. 16:3–12
Feb. 18 — Timothy to Teach Sound Doctrine. 1 Tim. 1:3–11
Feb. 19 — Speak Out for the Lord. 2 Tim. 1:8–14
Feb. 20 — Be Strong for the Lord. Eph. 6:10–20
Feb. 21 — Be True to God's Call. 1 Cor. 1:26–31
Feb. 22 — Timothy's Mission. 2 Tim. 3:1–10
Feb. 23 — Defend the Faith. 2 Tim. 3:10–17

Proclaim the Gospel!

1 Thessalonians 2:1–13

Persecution, suffering, death. Believers experience the dark side of life. What tools and resources does God give you to face such crisis times? Three New Testament books focus on these themes, so we will spend the next three months focusing on them: 1 Thessalonians, 2 Thessalonians, and Revelation. The goal of our focus is to bring us *hope for the future.* As I begin writing these lessons, I need hope for the present. I pray that God will give me new vision concerning these books of vision, for I stand on study ground where I feel more insecure than on that of any other biblical books. May God's hope strengthen me as I write and you as you study.

THE BIBLE LESSON

1 For yourselves, brethren, know our entrance in unto you, that it was not in vain:

2 But even after that we had suffered before, and were shamefully entreated, as ye know, at Philippi, we were bold in our God to speak unto you the gospel of God with much contention.

3 For our exhortation was not of deceit, nor of uncleanness, nor in guile:

4 But as we were allowed of God to be put in trust with the gospel, even so we speak; not as pleasing men, but God, which trieth our hearts.

5 For neither at any time used we flattering words, as ye know, nor a cloak of covetousness; God is witness:

6 Nor of men sought we glory, neither of you, nor yet of others, when we might have been burdensome, as the apostles of Christ.

7 But we were gentle among you, even as a nurse cherisheth her children:

8 So being affectionately desirous of you, we were willing to have imparted unto you, not the gospel of God only, but also our own souls, because ye were dear unto us.

9 For ye remember, brethren, our labour and travail: for labouring night and day, because we would not be chargeable unto any of you, we preached unto you the gospel of God.

10 Ye are witnesses, and God also, how holily and justly and unblameably we behaved ourselves among you that believe:

11 As ye know how we exhorted and comforted and charged every one of you, as a father doth his children,

12 That ye would walk worthy of God, who hath called you unto his kingdom and glory.

13 For this cause also thank we God without ceasing, because, when ye received the word of God which ye heard of us, ye received it not as the word of men, but as it is in truth, the word of God, which effectually worketh also in you that believe.

THE LESSON EXPLAINED

Proclaim Despite Persecution (2:1–4)

Bad memories die hard. Thessalonica provided plenty of bad memories for Paul. Jewish persecutors forced him to flee the city by night (Acts 17:10). Thessalonican persecutors followed him to Berea and forced him to flee again (Acts 17:13–14). Shortly thereafter, Paul wrote the first letter we have from him. He addressed the Thessalonian church with an extended thanksgiving for their faithfulness to the gospel and to him. Then he faced the problem head-on: To attack me is to attack the gospel I preach. You have to trust me to believe the gospel I bring is true. How do I defend myself? I lead you to defend me. You Thessalonians remember. We suffered at Philippi before we came to you (see Acts 16). Still we did not let that stop us. We preached the gospel boldly to you. And it succeeded. It did not fail, despite all the opposition we faced there. Our gospel brought you to know Christ. Why? Because we preached the way God wants us to preach. We did not deceive you. We did not preach human errors but divine truth. We did not try to trick you. Our motives were pure. We worked for a living and did not try to get money out of you. We did it God's way to please God.

Proclaim from Personal Passion (2:5–8)

What is God's way? A way that gives God's whole truth without seeking to make it fit popular opinion. A way without personal greed for money or popularity. A way that does not seek praise from people. A way that does not assert personal office and authority or demand payment for preaching services rendered. A way of gentle, caring love that a mother shows for a newborn infant she is nursing. A way of personal delight and love that shares one's own soul. A way not of personal gain but of personal passion for the gospel. That is God's way of proclamation.

Proclaim Through Perfect Living (2:9–13)

God's way of love and personal passion changes my lifestyle. I work day and night to help you and to earn a living for myself without burdening you. It is a way of high morality so no one can point the finger of blame my way. It preaches the truth even if that means correcting your lifestyle like a loving father would correct his children. It is a way with one goal: to be worthy of God's presence, God's calling, God's kingdom. It is a way that shows God's glory to the world. It is the way that led you to hear the gospel, believe the gospel, know the gospel was God's truth, and experience the gospel changing your lives. You are witnesses. The gospel won out in your life, the gospel you heard us proclaim. Now decide: the gospel we preach or the stories our enemies tell?

TRUTHS TO LIVE BY

The gospel makes enemies. People who do not believe the gospel find the gospel would destroy their lifestyle. They cannot be neutral to the gospel. They do everything in their power to defeat the gospel and to destroy the reputation of those who proclaim the gospel.

The gospel changes lives. The gospel is God's truth. It does more than add to your knowledge. It makes you behave differently. Greed, pride, envy, trickery leave your life. Love, concern, boldness, unselfishness, total devotion to God and His people mark your new life in Christ.

The gospel calls for proclamation. To know the gospel is to preach the gospel. The gospel grips everyone's life, not just the church officers'. If you believe the gospel, if you let the gospel take hold and control your life, you will be preaching the gospel. You will need no defense witnesses to prove you right. People you tell the gospel to will flock to defend you because they will see the gospel in your life.

A VERSE TO REMEMBER

But even after that we had suffered before, and were shamefully entreated, as ye know, at Philippi, we were bold in our God to speak unto you the gospel of God with much contention.—1 Thessalonians 2:2

DAILY BIBLE READINGS

Feb. 24 — Serve the True God. 1 Thess. 1:1–10
Feb. 25 — Witness of the Prophets. 1 Peter 1:1–10
Feb. 26 — Confess Jesus Christ. Rom. 10:1–13
Feb. 27 — Be Guardians of God's Word. Acts 20:26–38
Feb. 28 — Keep Your Ministry Honest. 1 Cor. 4:1–6
Mar. 1 — Make Your Message Clear. 1 Cor. 14:20–25
Mar. 2 — All People Should Praise God. Ps. 67:1–7

Live in Love and Holiness

1 Thessalonians 3:12–4:12

My next-door neighbor's son recently taught our church a lesson. Morgan regularly joins his father in our Wednesday night "Room at the Inn" program, providing food and shelter for homeless men. While there, the men get a trip to the clothes closet to finish out their meager wardrobe. One Wednesday night Morgan walked gingerly out to the car and met his Dad. "Where are your shoes, Morgan?" Dad asked suspiciously.

"One of the men was looking for a pair of size 9's. I had just looked and knew we did not have any, so I gave him mine," came the simple answer. "Humble" does not begin to describe the feeling of church-leader parents and neighbors. We had preached and taught love for the needy brother so long. Morgan practiced it.

■ THE BIBLE LESSON

12 And the Lord make you to increase and abound in love one toward another, and toward all men, even as we do toward you:

13 To the end he may stablish your hearts unblameable in holiness before God, even our Father, at the coming of our Lord Jesus Christ with all his saints.

....

1 Furthermore then we beseech you, brethren, and exhort you by the Lord Jesus, that as ye have received of us how ye ought to walk and to please God, so ye would abound more and more.

2 For ye know what commandments we gave you by the Lord Jesus.

3 For this is the will of God, even your sanctification, that ye should abstain from fornication:

4 That every one of you should know how to possess his vessel in sanctification and honour;

5 Not in the lust of concupiscence, even as the Gentiles which know not God:

6 That no man go beyond and defraud his brother in any matter: because that the Lord is the avenger of all such, as we also have forewarned you and testified.

7 For God hath not called us unto uncleanness, but unto holiness.

8 He therefore that despiseth, despiseth not man, but God, who hath also given unto us his holy Spirit.

9 But as touching brotherly love ye need not that I write unto you: for ye yourselves are taught of God to love one another.

10 And indeed ye do it toward all the brethren which are in all Macedonia: but we beseech you, brethren, that ye increase more and more;

11 And that ye study to be quiet, and to do your own business, and to work with your own hands, as we commanded you;

12 That ye may walk honestly toward them that are without, and that ye may have lack of nothing.

THE LESSON EXPLAINED

Prayer for Love (3:12–13)

Absence makes a missionary's heart grow fonder, too, especially when he hears good news about his new church's progress. Timothy brought such cheering news to Paul (3:6). This gave new energy to Paul's preaching (Acts 18:5) and praying (1 Thess. 3:10). He craved to return to Thessalonica (3:11; see 2:17–18), but God did not open that door. So he prayed, and what a prayer: Jesus, give them super abundant love for one another. Yes, Jesus, I pray to You as an equal with God. Make their love increase every day. But not just that, make them love everybody, even those people there who have been persecuting me and them. Make their love just like my love for them. Then Your purpose will be served, God. Their hearts will be steady on course. They will live holy lives, being holy like You are holy. They will be ready for Christ to return with His holy angels.

Call for Holiness (4:1-7)

Prayer to God needs support in words to people. Paul turned from his moment of prayer to a moment of exhortation. He begged the Thessalonians to put into practice what he had taught them and what they knew God wanted them to do. He placed special emphasis on sexual purity and fidelity to marriage vows: You have two examples, the pagan world and God's way. Which will direct your sexual habits?

Sexual behavior includes more than acts between a man and a woman. Other persons related to both parties are involved. Sexual sin betrays the trust other people put in you. It takes advantage of and exploits other people. You never have excuse as a Christian to take advantage of another person in sexual sin, in business practices, or in simple daily transactions. To do so is to invite God to judge you and avenge the wrong you have done. God has only one goal for you: holiness.

Example of Holiness (4:8-12)

Sexual sin or sin that takes advantage of another person is serious. It is sin against a person, but it is also sin against God. It indicates that you refuse to let the Holy Spirit (which God put in you to direct your life) do His work. You do not need another lesson in love. You need to do what you already know is right. You need to let the Spirit guide your life. You already love people. Look at all the witnesses throughout your state who can testify to that. Just don't get complacent. Don't be satisfied. Keep on loving more and more every day. Notice that love is sometimes silent. To love involves doing the business God has given you to do. It means work until Jesus comes again. Why? So those who do not believe will respect you and want to know the secret of your life and so no one else will have to supply needs you ought to supply for yourself. That shows you love all people: yourself, believers, and unbelievers.

TRUTHS TO LIVE BY

God expects two things from you. He expects you to love all people. He expects you to show love by living pure, holy lives that do not take advantage of anyone else and that gain the respect of other people.

God gives you two choices: Him or the pagan world. Someone will be your role model for living. You must choose. Act like the world, or act like God. Who is your model?

VERSES TO REMEMBER

And the Lord make you to increase and abound in love one toward another, and toward all men, even as we do toward you: To the end he may stablish your hearts unblameable in holiness before God, even our Father, at the coming of our Lord Jesus Christ with all his saints.
—1 Thessalonians 3:12–13

DAILY BIBLE READINGS

Mar. 3 — Love as God Loves. 1 Cor. 13:1–12
Mar. 4 — Live to Please God. Phil. 1:21–30
Mar. 5 — Seek the Mind of Christ. Phil. 2:1–8
Mar. 6 — Be Glad for Christian Obligations. Phil. 2:12–18
Mar. 7 — Promote Christian Conversations. Eph. 5:1–11
Mar. 8 — Serve Others As If Serving God. 1 Pet. 4:1–11
Mar. 9 — Love One Another Sincerely. 1 Pet. 1:13–22

Pray for Others!

2 Thessalonians 1

Wanda is a prayer warrior. Finding time to be a prayer warrior is not easy for this lovely widow. Her daily job buries her in stress. Yet Wanda knows her gifts. God has called her to a ministry of prayer. When someone in our church needs God in a special way, many call Wanda immediately. Others like me do not look for the emergency situation. We want to be on Wanda's prayer list permanently. When Wanda prays, things happen. Do not ask me to explain it. I just know that somehow we all see God at work in our lives when Wanda prays for us. Why? Wanda takes the Bible seriously. She prays always.

THE BIBLE LESSON

1 Paul, and Silvanus, and Timotheus, unto the church of the Thessalonians in God our Father and the Lord Jesus Christ:

2 Grace unto you, and peace, from God our Father and the Lord Jesus Christ.

3 We are bound to thank God always for you, brethren, as it is meet, because that your faith groweth exceedingly, and the charity of every one of you all toward each other aboundeth;

4 So that we ourselves glory in you in the churches of God for your patience and faith in all your persecutions and tribulations that ye endure:

5 Which is a manifest token of the righteous judgment of God, that ye may be counted worthy of the kingdom of God, for which ye also suffer:

6 Seeing it is a righteous thing with God to recompense tribulation to them that trouble you;

7 And to you who are troubled rest with us, when the Lord Jesus shall be revealed from heaven with his mighty angels,

8 In flaming fire taking vengeance on them that know not God, and that obey not the gospel of our Lord Jesus Christ:

9 Who shall be punished with everlasting destruction from the presence of the Lord, and from the glory of his power;

10 When he shall come to be glorified in his saints, and to be admired in all them that believe (because our testimony among you was believed) in that day.

11 Wherefore also we pray always for you that our God would count you worthy of this calling, and fulfil all the good pleasure of his goodness, and the work of faith with power:

12 That the name of our Lord Jesus Christ may be glorified in you, and ye in him, according to the grace of our God and the Lord Jesus Christ.

THE LESSON EXPLAINED

Pray in Thanksgiving (1:1–3)

Thanksgiving is not an option. You ought to do it. Thanksgiving is the fitting way of life for Christians as they relate to the church. Paul always followed the introduction of his letter with a thanksgiving for those to whom he wrote. He saw faith growing and love showing in the Thessalonican church. They grew in relation to God (faith) and others (love). He did not say thank you to them to flatter them or to get something out of them. They were doing what God asked in the first letter. So he gave thanks. What in your church is reason to thank God?

Pray for the Judgment Day (1:4–10)

Faith grew despite problems. People in Thessalonica had persecuted Paul. Now they persecuted the church Paul started. This made the church think they were enduring the last days. Judgment Day would come soon. Certainly persecution meant some people needed God's judgment. Faithfulness in persecution meant some needed the rewards of the Judgment Day. The faithful church is a church ready for judgment and worthy of taking part in God's kingdom now and hereafter. They suffered for the kingdom's sake and would participate in it. But what a horrible thought judgment is for those not suffering for the kingdom. They face God's zealous vengeance because they do not obey the gospel. They must live in eternity outside the presence of God, having no hope ever to see God. They will never see signs of God's glorious power. They will never experience the joy of life among the saints with God in glory. They will suffer eternal punishment. Pray to be faithful for the Judgment Day.

Pray for Christ's Glory (1:11–12)

Judgment Day praying is not selfish praying. You must include prayers for the church. Pray that each member will be faithful, that God will count each church member worthy of participating in the kingdom. Pray that each member will continue to grow in faith, that each may be prepared when persecution and suffering come. Most of all, pray that the church will bring glory, honor, fame, and marvelous reputation to Jesus Christ. This can only happen when God's grace keeps on working in you and in your church. Pray that it will. Pray always for the church.

TRUTHS TO LIVE BY

Prayer includes constant thanksgiving. Prayer looks outside oneself to see the great faith of others and rejoices with God in the faithful lives of other Christians. Faith wants to see the relationship with God and with other people grow. Faith encourages this by giving thanks to God for others. Give thanks to God for your church.

Prayer includes pride in the church's readiness for judgment. Churches with faith oppose the world with its doubt. Prayer is proud of the church's stand and expresses that pride to God. Prayer knows that faithful endurance in hard times signifies a relationship with God that guarantees you will be part of the kingdom on Judgment Day. Give glory to God.

Prayer includes glory for Christ. Prayer never focuses on earth and self. Prayer focuses on God, Christ, the kingdom, and the needs of others. Prayer sees God in action through His people and asks God to bring glory to Christ through everything the church does. Pray for the church to forget self and glorify Christ.

■ A VERSE TO REMEMBER

Wherefore also we pray always for you, that our God would count you worthy of this calling, and fulfill all the good pleasure of his goodness, and the work of faith with power.
—2 Thessalonians 1:11

■ DAILY BIBLE READINGS

Mar. 10 — Pray in Humility. 1 Chron. 7:12–18
Mar. 11 — Pray as Jesus Prayed. John 17:6–12
Mar. 12 — Pray in Private. Matt. 6:5–15
Mar. 13 — Pray in the Holy Spirit. Jude 17–23
Mar. 14 — Pray for the Sick. James 5:13–16
Mar. 15 — Pray for Friends. Acts 8:14–24
Mar. 16 — Pray for the Penitent. 1 Sam. 12:19–25

Do What Is Right!

2 Thessalonians 3:1–16

Missionary work created a major moral crisis for me. It brought moral freedom. Away from all the people I knew, in a foreign land, in a church and culture who lived by different moral standards than we did in the Bible belt, I faced a decision. Would I become like the new culture with its sophisticated moral freedom? Or would I be true to who I was and what I believed God wanted me to do? Thanks be to God that He gave my wife and me faith to follow His way, but I did learn that moral decision making can be tough when you leave the cultural security blanket of family, friends, and church. Sadly, our nation has thrown that moral security blanket away. Is our society any better than the Greek and Roman society the Thessalonians faced?

■ THE BIBLE LESSON

1 Finally, brethren, pray for us, that the word of the Lord may have free course, and be glorified, even as it is with you:

2 And that we may be delivered from unreasonable and wicked men: for all men have not faith.

3 But the Lord is faithful, who shall stablish you, and keep you from evil.

4 And we have confidence in the Lord touching you, that ye both do and will do the things which we command you.

5 And the Lord direct your hearts into the love of God, and into the patient waiting for Christ.

6 Now we command you, brethren, in the name of our Lord Jesus Christ, that ye withdraw yourselves from every brother that walketh disorderly, and not after the tradition which he received of us.

7 For yourselves know how ye ought to follow us: for we behaved not ourselves disorderly among you;

8 Neither did we eat any man's bread for nought; but wrought with labour and travail night and day, that we might not be chargeable to any of you:

9 Not because we have not power, but to make ourselves an ensample unto you to follow us.

10 For even when we were with you, this we commanded you, that if any would not work, neither should he eat.

11 For we hear that there are some which walk among you disorderly, working not at all, but are busybodies.

12 Now them that are such we command and exhort by our Lord Jesus Christ, that with quietness they work, and eat their own bread.

13 But ye, brethren, be not weary in well-doing.

14 And if any man obey not our word by this epistle, note that man, and have no company with him, that he may be ashamed.

15 Yet count him not as an enemy, but admonish him as a brother.

16 Now the Lord of peace himself give you peace always by all means. The Lord be with you all.

■ THE LESSON EXPLAINED

The Source of Right Living (3:1–5)

"How can you possibly obey God, Paul?" I have such a hard time. Temptations constantly plague me. It is hard. I need your prayers that I will do right. I know I must preach the gospel in hard places. Pray for me. Wicked people, unbelievers are out to get me. I face persecution if I do right. Pray for me. You can do right. I know you can. God is the source for doing right. He is trustworthy. You can count on Him to help you do right. God will do two things for you. He will give you His kind of love to love Him and His people. He will give you patience to know that the goal is worth the effort. Christ is coming. God will give you patience to do right while you wait. Trust the Source of right living.

The Example of Right Living (3:6–9)

"So few do right. I see people all around doing wrong. What can I do? Where is an example to follow?" Get out of the crowd that does wrong. Don't let yourself get caught up in continual temptation. We set the example for you. You can testify to the way we lived among you. You can live that way, too. We took advantage of no one. We worked for what we got. We did not cost you anything. We could have asked you for help, but we chose not to so you would have an example. Do right like we have done right. Are you a model for someone else to do right? Do you need to pray for God to send you a model of someone who does right? Who is the Paul in your midst?

The Discipline of Right Living (3:10–16)

Right living is not a gift someone gives you. It is a discipline you practice every day. People claim God is telling them to quit working because Jesus is coming. You know better. God never taught that. If you do not work, then you do not eat. Simple as that. What do you do when you quit working for a living? You start gossiping for recreation. Shut your mouths and get to work. Earn your bread and eat it. Then find ways to help others. Never get tired of helping other people. The same question again? "So few are doing right. How do we treat those who do wrong?" Isolate people who refuse to obey Jesus. Do not let them bring shame on you. Let them see how others react to them and become ashamed of themselves. Do this in love, not hate. Do it to help the busybody remember what the business of Jesus is. You need to discipline yourselves. You need to exercise discipline on others who refuse to discipline themselves. Do everything necessary to get the church to do right. Then you will know God's presence and God's peace.

■ TRUTHS TO LIVE BY

God has the power to help you do right. Do you give the world too much credit? Do you think the world's influence is so great you can never do right? You give God too little credit. God has the power to help you do right. You can obey because you have God's Spirit in your life. Let Him guide you to obey Him.

The church gives you examples of doing right. Are you so busy criticizing church hypocrites that you ignore church saints? Take your eyes off the wrongdoers long enough to find someone who will be your example of a right doer. Get in step with that person. If God can help that person obey, God can help you obey. Get together with that person. Learn to obey together. Help one another.

The church needs discipline. The church looks too much like the world, because the church is hungry for success instead of being hungry for righteousness. Will you and your church learn how to obey Christ in practicing self-discipline? in practicing church discipline?

■ A VERSE TO REMEMBER

But ye, brethren, be not weary in well-doing.
—2 Thessalonians 3:13

■ DAILY BIBLE READINGS

Mar. 17—Turn Away from Evil. Col. 3:1–10
Mar. 18—Do Everything in Jesus' Name. Col. 3:12–17
Mar. 19—Be Gracious to Others. Col. 4:1–5
Mar. 20—Live in Harmony with Others. Rom. 5:1–6
Mar. 21—Live Peaceably Within the Church. Eph. 4:1–8
Mar. 22—Live Peacefully Within the Family. Eph. 4:25–32
Mar. 23—Rules for Christian Living. 1 Pet. 3:8–12

The Resurrection Hope

Matthew 28:1–10; 1 Thessalonians 4:13-18

Last Saturday night a five-month-old baby quit breathing. Parents rushed the child to the hospital. Doctors and nurses worked around the clock to save the child's life. Churches began prayer vigils. Sunday School class ministered to the family in every way possible. Monday the child died. Shock! Grief! Sorrow! Anger! Frustration! Fear! Doubt! All the emotions set in. People in our church joined hundreds of others in the community asking the obvious question: why? Of course, no one can answer, only ask. The one thing certain from the experience: we see again why we need and cherish the resurrection hope. Unfathomable death requires Easter.

■ THE BIBLE LESSON

MATTHEW 28

1 In the end of the sabbath, as it began to dawn toward the first day of the week, came Mary Magdalene and the other Mary to see the sepulchre.

2 And, behold, there was a great earthquake: for the angel of the Lord descended from heaven, and came and rolled back the stone from the door, and sat upon it.

3 His countenance was like lightning, and his raiment white as snow:

4 And for fear of him the keepers did shake, and became as dead men.

5 And the angel answered and said unto the women, Fear not ye: for I know that ye seek Jesus, which was crucified.

6 He is not here: for he is risen, as he said. Come, see the place where the Lord lay.

7 And go quickly, and tell his disciples that he is risen from the dead; and, behold, he goeth before you into Galilee; there shall ye see him: lo, I have told you.

8 And they departed quickly from the sepulchre with fear and great joy; and did run to bring his disciples word.

9 And as they went to tell his disciples, behold, Jesus met them, saying, All hail. And they came and held him by the feet, and worshipped him.

10 Then said Jesus unto them, Be not afraid: go tell my brethren that they go into Galilee, and there shall they see me.

....

1 THESSALONIANS 4

13 But I would not have you to be ignorant, brethren, concerning them which are asleep, that ye sorrow not, even as others which have no hope.

14 For if we believe that Jesus died and rose again, even so them also which sleep in Jesus will God bring with him.

15 For this we say unto you by the word of the Lord, that we which are alive and remain unto the coming of the Lord shall not prevent them which are asleep.

16 For the LORD himself shall descend from heaven with a shout, with the voice of the archangel, and with the trump of God: and the dead in Christ shall rise first:

17 Then we which are alive and remain shall be caught up together with them in the clouds, to meet the LORD in the air: and so shall we ever be with the LORD.

18 Wherefore comfort one another with these words.

■ THE LESSON EXPLAINED

The Resurrection Event (Matt. 28:1-10)

Hopes so high, now destroyed. He talked so much about the kingdom, but the emperor got Him. I thought if anyone could beat the Roman system, He could do it. He made fools out of our religious leaders. His miracles showed He had more power than anyone ever had. His prayer time showed God directed every step He took. And He was so loving. Then, this! How could He die? Why? At least we can show our respect to the dead and put incense on the body like we are supposed to. Wait! What's happening? The earth trembles. Look at His tomb. The guards are on the ground. Someone's there, all bright and white and shining. Who is it? What's happening?

Do not fear. You look for Jesus. He's not here. God raised Him from the dead. See where His body was. Give His disciples a message. Hurry up to Galilee. He'll meet them there.

Hurry! Let's go.

Hello, there.

It's Jesus. We can only fall to our knees, reach out to touch His feet, and worship. He said something. He, too, says go to Galilee. It's true. He is alive. Hope is not dead! Hurry! Tell!

The Resurrection Hope (1 Thess. 4:13–15)

He arose. Hundreds saw Him. He ascended to heaven. Twenty years later His gospel has spread through the Roman empire. What's wrong? Where is He? Why does He not come back? So many of our people are dying without seeing Him return? When will He come?

Do not worry. We are not trying to hide secret information from you. Do you truly believe Jesus died and God raised Him? Are you certain these who died believed in Jesus? Then no reason to worry. God will raise believers who have died when Jesus comes again, just as He will gather believers who still live. Your departed loved ones are safe in Christ. I know you grieve at losing them, but do not worry. The resurrection hope applies to them, too.

The Resurrection Return (1 Thess. 4:16–18)

What will happen when He returns? I cannot give you all the details. A brief summary should be enough to help you with your grieving. Christ will come again. The archangel and heavenly trumpets will make sure everyone knows. The dead will rise up first thing. Then Christ will gather the living believers to Himself in the clouds. We all, dead believers and living believers, will be together with Christ forever. These words you can share with one another when someone dies. Death is not the end. Death is not the winner. Christ is. He will return. He will take you to be with Him!

■ TRUTHS TO LIVE BY

God raised Jesus from the dead. The Easter story is the Christian story. Christianity has a gospel, good news, a right to exist only if God raised Jesus and emptied the tomb forever. Our hope is not that we can win doctrinal arguments. Our hope is that Jesus is alive and is coming for us.

Death is a grievous reality. We cannot escape death or hide its ugliness. Death comes to each. Death hurts the living. Grief and all its accompanying emotions are natural, necessary responses to death. No amount of funeral parlor make-up and courtesy can hide the ugly reality of death.

Resurrection is a joyous reality. God raised Jesus. He will raise all believers. Separated by death now, we will see one another again and enjoy fellowship together with Christ for eternity. That is why we have hope!

■ A VERSE TO REMEMBER

For if we believe that Jesus died and rose again, even so them also which sleep in Jesus will God bring with him.
—1 Thessalonians 4:14

■ DAILY BIBLE READINGS

Mar. 24 — Jesus Christ Died for Sinners. Rom. 5:1–11
Mar. 25 — God's Gift of Grace for All. Rom. 5:12–19
Mar. 26 — The Fact of the Resurrection. 1 Cor. 15:1–11
Mar. 27 — The Need for the Resurrection. 1 Cor. 15:12–19
Mar. 28 — The Assurance of the Resurrection.
  1 Cor. 15:20–28
Mar. 29 — The Nature of the Resurrection. 1 Cor. 15:35–44
Mar. 30 — The Victory of the Resurrection. 1 Cor. 15:51–58

Commanded to Write

Revelation 1:4–15

Revelation! The sound of the word rouses high expectations. New knowledge. Something other people do not know and I will. Mysteries, secrets. Revelation! It also rouses fears. What if I am left out and someone else gets the knowledge? What if I do not understand the message? Revelation! It also rouses arguments. I know the meaning better than you do. If you do not understand it the way I do, then you are not as good a Christian as I am. If you cannot talk about tribulation, rapture, and millennium, then you just cannot study the book. (See the *Disciple's Study Bible* [Broadman and Holman, 1988], pp. 1631–35 for outlines and charts to use in studying Revelation.)

Studying Revelation affects believers in many different ways. You have a right to know that your writer approaches the task with uncertainty and reverence. I do not have a developed system that helps explain all the secrets of the book. I seek simply to find clear teachings that you can apply as truths to live by.

■ THE BIBLE LESSON

4 John to the seven churches which are in Asia: Grace be unto you, and peace, from him which is, and which was, and which is to come; and from the seven Spirits which are before his throne;

5 And from Jesus Christ, who is the faithful witness, and the first begotten of the dead, and the prince of the kings of the earth. Unto him that loved us, and washed us from our sins in his own blood,

6 And hath made us kings and priests unto God and his Father; to him be glory and dominion for ever and ever. Amen.

7 Behold, he cometh with clouds; and every eye shall see him, and they also which pierced him: and all kindreds of the earth shall wail because of him. Even so, Amen.

8 I am Alpha and Omega, the beginning and the ending, saith the LORD, which is, and which was, and which is to come, the Almighty.

9 I John, who also am your brother, and companion in tribulation, and in the kingdom and patience of Jesus Christ, was in the isle that is called Patmos, for the word of God, and for the testimony of Jesus Christ.

10 I was in the Spirit on the LORD's day, and heard behind me a great voice, as of a trumpet,

11 Saying, I am Alpha and Omega, the first and the last: and, What thou seest, write in a book, and send it unto the seven churches which are in Asia; unto Ephesus, and unto Smyrna, and unto Pergamos, and unto Thyatira, and unto Sardis, and unto Philadelphia, and unto Laodicea.

12 And I turned to see the voice that spake with me. And being turned, I saw seven golden candlesticks;

13 And in the midst of the seven candlesticks one like unto the Son of man, clothed with a garment down to the foot, and girt about the paps with a golden girdle.

14 His head and his hairs were white like wool, as white as snow; and his eyes were as a flame of fire;

15 And his feet like unto fine brass, as if they burned in a furnace; and his voice as the sound of many waters.

THE LESSON EXPLAINED

Revelation Introduced (1:1–8)

What does the future hold? The immediate future? Our pastor is in prison? Jews are getting the government to arrest us. Leaders are being killed for the faith. Rome wants us to worship the emperor. Over sixty years have passed with no sign of Jesus coming back. Why should we remain faithful to Jesus and the church? It will cost us our social standing, our jobs, our lives. Give in to the government and have life easy.

A letter from our pastor! What does John have to say to us? He says he received a new revelation about Jesus from God. It tells about what God is about to do. God will bless us if we read this and obey it. It is not just for us. It is for the seven churches around us here in the Roman province of Asia. John writes in the power of the Trinitarian God, the eternal Father, full totally complete, seven-fold Spirit, and Jesus. He reminds us that Jesus was raised from the dead and is still ruler over all earthly kings. Jesus loves us. He died for us. He gained forgiveness for all our sins through His blood. We are kings and priests in His kingdom with a responsibility to serve Him and Him alone. God has a promise for us. Jesus will come again. He has not forgotten. We must be patient and wait until God sends Him back on the clouds. We will see Him, and His enemies will, too. They will cry in terror when He comes. He is eternal. Our enemies are not. Why are we so afraid?

Revelation Received (1:9–20)

Hear John's voice again. He received this revelation, but he does not feel like he is any better than we are. He is still our brother in Christ. He is suffering just as much if not more than we are. After all, he is isolated on that little, bitty island of Patmos, sixteen square miles of rock. They put him in prison for preaching, and he still writes letters, preaching to us. He still uses the Lord's Day as a day of worship, even in prison. He writes because the eternal God told him to. What we are about to read are God's words to us. God even gave John a vision of the One speaking to him. He saw seven lamps like those in the temple (1 Kings 8:49). He has seven lamps and seven churches. The lamps must represent our churches. The Son of man, that's Jesus, stood in the middle. Jesus stands in the middle of our churches. He is dressed just like the high priest. We have no need to fear. We have lost our pastor, but we still have Jesus our High Priest to speak to God for us and to speak to us for God. He looks just as He was described in Daniel 7. He holds our churches in His hand. His appearance scared John to death, but Jesus lifted him up and told him not to fear. Jesus wants us to know He is still alive and in charge. He controls everything, even death and hell. Surely we have no reason to be afraid.

Jesus has come to tell us about the future. We need to read and listen carefully. He will give us hope.

■ TRUTHS TO LIVE BY

Life brings fear. Every generation faces some reason to fear worldly powers and forsake Jesus. We do not have to look far to see someone who wants to control us and threatens us if we do not forget Jesus and do what this person says. How you handle fear of the world says a lot about who you are.

Fear not is the Bible's basic message. God wants you to live in peace, not in fear. He speaks through the prophets, through Jesus, through Paul, through John, and through worship to tell you to throw away your fears. You have two ways you can face life: with fear, or with faith in Jesus. Choose one today.

You can face the future without fear. If the present is bad, the future seems only worse. Imagination builds horrid images of what may come tomorrow. Jesus knows your fears. He gives you the book of Revelation to calm your fears and show you He controls the world's future and your future. If you believe Him, you have no reason to fear the future.

■ A VERSE TO REMEMBER

What thou seest, write in a book, and send it unto the seven churches. . . .—Revelation 1:11a

■ DAILY BIBLE READINGS

Mar. 31 — Jesus, God's Eternal Word. John 1:1–8
Apr. 1 — Jesus, the Light of the World. John 1:9–18
Apr. 2 — We Live Through Jesus Christ. Rom. 6:1–11
Apr. 3 — Christ, the Head of All Things. Col. 1:15–23
Apr. 4 — Give Thanks to the Lord. Ps. 100
Apr. 5 — God Honors Those Who Serve Him. John 12:20–26
Apr. 6 — A Savior for All People. Luke 2:25–33

To Smyrna and Pergamum

Revelation 2:8–17

False doctrine is no laughing matter. The mention of Waco, Texas, reminds us of that. Adolph Hitler should have taught us that long ago. False doctrine is dangerous because it leads to fanatical false practice. People suffer and die because people defend falsehood in the name of truth. You and I may tend to laugh at false doctrine and wonder how people could so foolishly belief it and trust its crazy leaders. The resurrected Jesus took false doctrine seriously. You need to find the one word He calls out to you when false doctrine enters your life.

■ THE BIBLE LESSON

8 And unto the angel of the church in Smyrna write; These things saith the first and the last, which was dead, and is alive;

9 I know thy works, and tribulation, and poverty, (but thou art rich) and I know the blasphemy of them which say they are Jews, and are not, but are the synagogue of Satan.

10 Fear none of those things which thou shalt suffer: behold, the devil shall cast some of you into prison, that ye may be tried; and ye shall have tribulation ten days: be thou faithful unto death, and I will give thee a crown of life.

11 He that hath an ear, let him hear what the Spirit saith unto the churches; He that overcometh shall not be hurt of the second death.

12 And to the angel of the church in Pergamos write; These things saith he which hath the sharp sword with two edges;

13 I know thy works, and where thou dwellest, even where Satan's seat is: and thou holdest fast my name, and hast not denied my faith, even in those days wherein Antipas was my faithful martyr, who was slain among you, where Satan dwelleth.

14 But I have a few things against thee, because thou hast there them that hold the doctrine of Balaam, who taught Balac to cast a stumblingblock before the children of Israel, to eat things sacrificed unto idols, and to commit fornication.

15 So hast thou also them that hold the doctrine of the Nicolaitans, which thing I hate.

16 Repent; or else I will come unto thee quickly, and will fight against them with the sword of my mouth.

17 He that hath an ear, let him hear what the Spirit saith unto the churches; To him that overcometh will I give to eat of the hidden manna, and will give him a white stone, and in the stone a new name written, which no man knoweth saving he that receiveth it.

■ THE LESSON EXPLAINED

Faithful unto Death (2:8–11)

Seven letters open the book of Revelation. These keep the book firmly anchored in history, in the life of local churches, and in the needs of real people. Letters describing church needs precede visions showing God's solution to those needs. The letters have a pattern: (1) write to the angel of the church; (2) identify Christ the author with a phrase from chapter 1; (3) positive achievements of the local church; (4) encouragement, censure, counsel, and/or warning; (5) an exhortation to hear; and (6) promise to the faithful.

Smyrna was a rich, Aegean seaport city, (modern Izmir, the only one of the seven still existing) of perhaps 200,000 people. Noted for its strong ties to the Roman government, it also had a large Jewish population. These Jews apparently spied on the Christians and tried to get the government to persecute the church. Dying for faith in Christ was a reality in Smyrna. Christ identified with them as the One who had been killed but had risen and was alive. He knew the church well, had not forgotten them. They complained of poverty in a rich city. He reminded them they had the riches of God's kingdom even as they suffered. The Jews persecuting them had no claims as God's people. Such people belonged to Satan, not to God. Hope lies not in success in this world. Smyrna faced more persecution and death, but they should never fear. Christ had eternal life for them. Only those sentenced in the final judgment had reason to fear. Christians should be faithful and live forever.

Repent of False Doctrine (2:12–17)

Pergamum was a political and religious capital. Its library boasted 200,000 volumes. People flocked to its temples of Zeus, Athene, Dionysos, and Asklepios, the god of healing. The city prided itself as the first city to be allowed to build a temple to the emperor. This made it the seat of Satan, where the satanic emperor was worshiped. Rome granted its ruler permission to kill anyone he chose. Against him stood Christ with the two-edged sword, equipped to destroy any human ruler. This Christ congratulated the church for its faithfulness even as its leader was killed. He censured them of false doctrine seeping in. Some members, called both followers of Balaam (see Num. 25:1; 2 Pet. 2:15) and Nicolaitans (see Rev. 2:6 and possibly 2:20–25), tempted the church to a "both/and" practice: Appease Rome. Participate in emperor worship. Doff your hats to the pagan gods. Even eat the sacrifices given them. If you want to, enjoy the sexual rituals of these gods. As long as you do not really believe in this stuff, it does not matter what you do. Be cooperative and save your neck. For such giving in to wrong, Jesus has one word: Repent. My sword can get you, too. Repent, I will supply your needs and admit you to My source of eternal food.

■ TRUTHS TO LIVE BY

The Bible does not promise success. Opposition, persecution, death are the world's rewards for those who give all to Christ. Jesus never promised anything less.

The Bible does not allow compromise. Pretending obedience to false religion to save your scalp brings Christ's wrath. Jesus never gives permission to do what is wrong in the name of safety. He calls to faithfulness even if it costs your life.

The Bible promises eternal life for the faithful. The Bible's hope is for life eternal after the resurrection. Christ's presence will lead you through present trouble. His promise of eternal life will motivate you to faithfulness.

■ A VERSE TO REMEMBER

Be thou faithful unto death, and I will give thee a crown of life.—Revelation 2:10

■ DAILY BIBLE READINGS

Apr. 7 — Repent and Return to God. Acts 3:17–26
Apr. 8 — Pray for Spiritual Wisdom. Col. 1:9–14
Apr. 9 — Overcome by Faith. 1 John 5:1–5
Apr. 10 — Have Faith in Jesus Christ. 1 John 5:6–12
Apr. 11 — Hold Firm Your Hope. Heb. 3:1–6
Apr. 12 — Be Wise in the Lord. Prov. 4:1–9
Apr. 13 — Be Faithful and Righteous. Prov. 28:20–28

To Thyatira

Revelation 2:18–29

God is not as you think. He is love and goodness. He would never punish you or hurt you. He wants you to enjoy life and have the best life can offer. He would never take away from you the best things of life. Don't let those traditional fools down at the church rob you of fun and excitement. Come join me. Worship God the way I do, the fun and success way. This is real religion. This is the true God. This is the way God wants you to live. See how good He has been to me. He will do the same for you.

What an alluring spiel some preachers have! How do you know who is right and who is wrong? How do you tell which one describes God in the right way? You have the same questions the people at Thyatira had.

■ THE BIBLE LESSON

18 And unto the angel of the church in Thyatira write; These things saith the Son of God, who hath his eyes like unto a flame of fire, and his feet are like fine brass;

19 I know thy works, and charity, and service, and faith, and thy patience, and thy works; and the last to be more than the first.

20 Notwithstanding I have a few things against thee, because thou sufferest that woman Jezebel, which calleth herself a prophetess, to teach and to seduce my servants to commit fornication, and to eat things sacrificed unto idols.

21 And I gave her space to repent of her fornication; and she repented not.

22 Behold, I will cast her into a bed, and them that commit adultery with her into great tribulation, except they repent of their deeds.

23 And I will kill her children with death; and all the churches shall know that I am he which searcheth the reins and hearts: and I will give unto every one of you according to your works.

24 But unto you I say, and unto the rest in Thyatira, as many as have not this doctrine, and which have not known the depths of Satan, as they speak; I will put upon you none other burden.

25 But that which ye have already hold fast till I come.

26 And he that overcometh, and keepeth my works unto the end, to him will I give power over the nations:

27 And he shall rule them with a rod of iron; as the vessels of a potter shall they be broken to shivers: even as I received of my Father.

28 And I will give him the morning star.

29 He that hath an ear, let him hear what the Spirit saith unto the churches.

THE LESSON EXPLAINED

Praise for Faith and Works (2:18–19)

You are not all bad. I, Jesus, know the good things you are doing. My eyes can see everything. I stand firm, not wavering from one opinion to another. I am proud of the way you minister in My name. You live in a city noted for its labor force, its trade guilds, its fine products created by excellent craftsmen. But to be a member of a trade guild is to join in pagan worship. What do you do? You have been patient. You have shown love for me and one another. You have kept the faith. I am proud of you.

Judgment for False Religion (2:20–23)

Not all of you, however. You face a major temptation. This seductive, charming woman among you is really a Jezebel (see 1 Kings 16; 2 Kings 9). She claims to be My prophet. You folks allow her to remain in the church and teach My people. You let her lead the people into pagan worship and pagan sexual rites. Then you let her come back and worship with you. I have tried every way to get her to repent. She will not. Her death bed is near as is persecution for all who follow her. You will receive what your sins deserve. Watch out. Repent now, or else.

Promise for the Faithful (2:24–29)

Don't worry. I am not talking to all of you. Most have not followed this Jezebel. I am not trying to add to your burdens. Just keep on being obedient and experiencing My presence as you have been doing. It will all prove worthwhile in the end. Then I will give to you My power to rule the nations. The nations that cause you so much trouble now and tempt you to worship the emperor or to join your employer and fellow employees in pagan worship—all these will be punished and broken (see Ps. 2:8–9). Do not worry about them. I will give you all you need. Just pay attention to what I say. Keep the faith.

■ TRUTHS TO LIVE BY

God knows what you are up to. Your faithfulness day by day may seem to go unnoticed and unrewarded. Bad days make you ask, is it worth it? Christ assures you that He knows every last thing you do for Him. The reward is coming.

God knows the temptations you face. Evil seems so strong and wins every one else to its cause. People gain business promotions, new jobs, social status, wealth, everything because they give in to a few temptations. Why, they even remain church leaders. Why not you? Because Christ has set a time for your reward and their punishment. Keep on being patient and obey.

God will make it all worthwhile in the end. Today's problems blind us to tomorrow's hope. Christ knows every difficulty you face. He knows how hard it is to survive day to day. He asks you to keep on keeping on. Do not give up. Life may seem dark today, but His morning star rises tomorrow. He already has a reward planned for you. Stick with Him, and receive the reward.

■ A VERSE TO REMEMBER

And I will kill her children with death; and all the churches shall know that I am he which searcheth the reins and hearts: and I will give unto every one of you according to your works.—Revelation 2:23

■ DAILY BIBLE READINGS

Apr. 14 — God Searches Our Hearts. Rom. 8:26–30
Apr. 15 — God Shows No Partiality. Rom. 2:1–11
Apr. 16 — God Rewards According to Works. Ps. 62:8–12
Apr. 17 — God Rescues the Godly from Trial. 2 Pet. 2:4–10
Apr. 18 — Hold Fast to Freedom in Christ. Gal. 5:1–14
Apr. 19 — Rejoice in the Lord. Phil. 4:1–9
Apr. 20 — Test Your Faith. 2 Cor. 13:5–10

To Philadelphia and Laodicea
Revelation 3:7–22

He drives the streets of the city in limousines, telling drivers what to do and when. People wrestle one another for a sight of him. Reporters quote almost anything they hear him say—when it is printable. He gives lavishly to charities and religious organizations. He has life under control. He is much like the Laodiceans. Then Christ knocks on the door. What then?

■ THE BIBLE LESSON

7 And to the angel of the church in Philadelphia write; These things saith he that is holy, he that is true, he that hath the key of David, he that openeth, and no man shutteth; and shutteth, and no man openeth;

8 I know thy works: behold, I have set before thee an open door, and no man can shut it: for thou hast a little strength, and hast kept my word, and hast not denied my name.

9 Behold, I will make them of the synagogue of Satan, which say they are Jews, and are not, but do lie; behold, I will make them to come and worship before thy feet, and to know that I have loved thee.

10 Because thou hast kept the word of my patience, I also will keep thee from the hour of temptation, which shall come upon all the world, to try them that dwell upon the earth.

. . . .

15 I know thy works, that thou art neither cold nor hot: I would thou wert cold or hot.

16 So then because thou art lukewarm, and neither cold nor hot, I will spue thee out of my mouth.

17 Because thou sayest, I am rich, and increased with goods, and have need of nothing; and knowest not that thou art wretched, and miserable, and poor, and blind, and naked:

18 I counsel thee to buy of me gold tried in the fire, that thou mayest be rich; and white raiment, that thou mayest be clothed, and that the shame of thy nakedness do not appear; and anoint thine eyes with eye-salve, that thou mayest see.

19 As many as I love, I rebuke and chasten: be zealous therefore, and repent.

20 Behold, I stand at the door, and knock: if any man hear my voice, and open the door, I will come in to him, and will sup with him, and he with me.

21 To him that overcometh will I grant to sit with me in my throne, even as I also overcame, and am set down with my Father in his throne.

■ THE LESSON EXPLAINED

The Power of a Little Strength (3:7–13)

Grape and wine industry, location on a major imperial trade route, and geographical setting as the gateway to the east made Philadelphia a strong and proud city. The church, however, was weak and apparently insignificant. Jews opposed it. Pagans opposed it. Nothing seemed to be happening. Christ came with praise, and only praise. No condemnation. The Holy One knows the church, its weakness, its possibilities, and its faith. The church steadfastly held to Christ and His teaching despite the world's temptations and powers. Christ rewards such patient obedience with the power to resist the even-greater temptations and trials approaching. Only Christ can admit people to God's kingdom, and He has them first in line for admission. He would write on them all the names needed for entrance. Who would have the power then?

The Weakness of Indecision (3:14–16)

Bankers, sheep breeders, doctors, teachers, and other wealthy citizens proudly walked the streets of Laodicea, a city proud of its wealth and power. A church nestled securely among its streets, its members apparently proud of nothing and committed to nothing. One goal sufficed for them: stay in existence just like we are, rich and indifferent. Jesus came with nothing good to say about the self-satisfied, uncommitted church. Stand up for something, He said, or give up all together.

The Waste of a Life of Wealth (3:17–22)

You have let your wealth deceive you. You see nothing that you need. I see everything you need. You must face the choice: your resources or My resources. Which will it be? You are proud of Laodicea's rich banks, black wool, and special medical salves. You need to be looking for the kind of wealth I give, the clothing fit for My kingdom, and the healing ointments I provide. Don't turn me off. Listen. I would not talk to you if I did not love you. Calling you to change shows how much I care. You have closed the door and shut Me out of your church. Listen. Get excited about something, about Me and My kingdom. Repent before it is too late. The opportunity remains. I stand knocking at your door. Will you invite Me back in? Does My presence and fellowship mean anything to you? Look at the choice once more: your self-satisfied wealth or share the throne in My kingdom? Are you listening?

■ TRUTHS TO LIVE BY

Outward appearances are deceiving. Philadelphia appeared weak and helpless. Laodicea appeared strong and rich. Jesus applauded Philadelphia's strength and pointed out Laodicea's poverty. How do you measure yourself and your church? Are you as well off and secure as you think you are?

Christ has the only resources you need. Food, clothing, housing, transportation, recreation, investments. We quickly and easily list what we just have to have to make it in this world. Christ has a different list. Do you want earthly resources or eternal resources?

Christ gives you one more chance. You are a church member. Christ writes His letters to you. He asks you to repent, to open the door, to let Him in, to know, enjoy, and value His presence. That is the only entrance to eternal security. Will you open the door and let Him in? Will you repent?

■ A VERSE TO REMEMBER

I know thy works.—Revelation 3:8, 15

■ DAILY BIBLE READINGS

Apr. 21 — Love One Another. 1 John 3:11–24
Apr. 22 — Listen to God's Call. Isa. 55:1–9
Apr. 23 — Expect Christ's Coming. 2 Thess. 1:5–10
Apr. 24 — Endure Trials to the End. Matt. 24:4–14
Apr. 25 — Trust God, Not Wealth. Prov. 10:11–24
Apr. 26 — Bless the Lord for His Care. Deut. 8:1–10
Apr. 27 — Do All for God's Glory. 1 Cor. 10:23–33

The Redeeming Lamb

Revelation 5:1–10

What is heaven like? John got to see. A door opened in heaven. A voice invited him in (4:1). Why? So John could see what the future held. Meanwhile, John watched heaven's worship service (4:11). In the spirit of heaven's worship God prepared John for the most amazing things a human being has ever seen. Revelation 5–21 unfold amazements one after another. When finished, John and the reader are exhausted from pleasure, from intense worship, from working to understand what has been seen, and from amazement at who God is and what He is doing. The entire process of revelation begins with the Star of the show: the Redeeming Lamb. Be ready to stand amazed in the presence.

■ THE BIBLE LESSON

1 And I saw in the right hand of him that sat on the throne a book written within and on the backside, sealed with seven seals.

2 And I saw a strong angel proclaiming with a loud voice, Who is worthy to open the book, and to loose the seals thereof?

3 And no man in heaven, nor in earth, neither under the earth, was able to open the book, neither to look thereon.

4 And I wept much, because no man was found worthy to open and to read the book, neither to look thereon.

5 And one of the elders saith unto me, Weep not: behold, the Lion of the tribe of Juda, the Root of David, hath prevailed to open the book, and to loose the seven seals thereof.

6 And I beheld, and, lo, in the midst of the throne and of the four beasts, and in the midst of the elders, stood a Lamb as it had been slain, having seven horns and seven eyes, which are the seven Spirits of God sent forth into all the earth.

7 And he came and took the book out of the right hand of him that sat upon the throne.

8 And when he had taken the book, the four beasts and four and twenty elders fell down before the Lamb, having every one of them harps, and golden vials full of odours, which are the prayers of saints.

9 And they sang a new song, saying, Thou art worthy to take the book, and to open the seals thereof: for thou wast slain, and hast redeemed us to God by thy blood out of every kindred, and tongue, and people, and nation;

10 And hast made us unto our God kings and priests: and we shall reign on the earth.

■ THE LESSON EXPLAINED

Heaven's Predicament (5:1–4)

God has a book, a huge book (see Dan. 12:4). He sits on the throne holding His book. What is a book for? To read, to understand, to act upon what it says. What a tragedy: You cannot open this book. It is sealed shut with seven seals. The heavenly angels want to open the book. They have established a search party. Who can find someone who can open God's book? In hell under the earth, no one can open it. On earth among humans no one can open it. Even in heaven no one can open it. They cannot even look at it. It is too holy. Alas! What a horrible predicament! Come, cry with me. God wants to give revelation, but no one is worthy even to look at the revelation, much less open it and read. What can we do?

Heaven's Savior (5:5–7)

Wait a minute. The heavenly elders, those seated nearest God's throne in the heavenly council, have found a solution. Listen to their spokesman. He wants to dry my tears. What is he pointing to? It is the Messiah, Jesus Himself, the Root grown up from the remnant of David (see Gen. 49:9,10; Isa. 11:1,10). He has taken the book. He has undone the seals. We can have God's perfect revelation from His book because the Lamb is there, the One who was killed (see John 1:29). He is no longer dead. He possesses the symbols of perfect power (seven horns) and of absolute knowledge (seven eyes). He has the total Spirit of God in Him. He knows everything happening in all the earth. He has the book!

Heaven's Reaction (5:8–10)

Heavenly worship breaks out again. Earth participates, too, for they have our prayers, letting them spill out into the heavens like perfume. No one listens to us on earth, but in heaven God knows our prayers. Listen, no song like this has ever been sung. The Lamb is worthy. Praise His name. He gave up His life. He endured the worst things earth could give Him. Why? So we could be saved. So our sins could be forgiven. He is our Redeemer (see Mark 10:45; 1 Cor. 6:20). Praise the Lamb. That applies to every one of us. His salvation goes across every barrier we humans can erect: race, nationality, language, geography. The Lamb broke down all barriers. Salvation is available to everyone through Him. Praise Jesus. We suffer now, but God has a different role for us. We will rule in His kingdom. We will be priests leading worship for Him (see Exod. 19:6). Listen. Worship is spreading. The angels join in. All the heavenly creatures, and those on earth, too, join in. What a marvelous day. The Lamb has God's book. We can know God's plan for the future. Jesus will tell it to us.

■ TRUTHS TO LIVE BY

You are not worthy to know God's revelation. God is holy. All He touches is holy. His plans are holy. You have no reason to expect to know anything about God or what God has planned for you. Anything you know is because God in His grace and love has chosen to make it known. It is because

Christ obediently died for you and is worthy to know God's plan and is loving to reveal those plans.

Jesus Christ died for your sins. The Bible has one central theme: God provided salvation for you through the death of Jesus Christ. Have you accepted that salvation by asking Jesus to forgive your sins? Have you confessed Jesus as your Savior and Lord?

Jesus alone is worthy of your worship. You can join the heavenly chorus. You can sing praise to Jesus. If you have repented of your sins and claimed Him as Savior and Lord, you will want nothing more than you want to worship Him. Praise Jesus.

■ A VERSE TO REMEMBER

Thou art worthy to take the book, and to open the seals thereof: for thou wast slain, and hast redeemed us to God by thy blood out of every kindred, and tongue, and people, and nation.—Revelation 5:9

■ DAILY BIBLE READINGS

Apr. 28 — The Lamb Sacrificed. Isa. 53:4–9
Apr. 29 — The Lamb Receives a Kingdom. Dan. 7:9–14
Apr. 30 — Sinners Ransomed by the Blood of Christ.
   1 Pet. 1:18–25
May 1 — The Lamb, the Light of Jerusalem.
   Rev. 21:22–27
May 2 — The Lamb, Worthy of Praise. Rev. 4:1–11
May 3 — The Redeemed Worshiped the Lamb.
   Rev. 14:1–5
May 4 — The Lamb, Our Final Judge. Rom. 14:1–11

Provision for the Redeemed

Revelation 7:1–17

My wife and I have just seen a stunning movie. A black man and a white man fight over control of a nuclear submarine while missiles are about to be launched. The fate of the universe seems to hang in the balance. In the end the black man wins, and with him justice prevails on earth, at least for a little while. But the issue is not black and white. The issue is power and how to use it. It is about the chain of command and who has authority. It is about universal peace and how to obtain it. John wrote a much more powerful drama on these same subjects. He uses symbols to show how God and His chain of command operate to use ultimate power to establish peace on earth forever. The Lamb opens the seals one by one (ch. 6; also see 8:1). They reveal the tribulations and persecutions the church faces on earth. The whole natural order of the universe breaks down. Now what?

■ THE BIBLE LESSON

1 And after these things I saw four angels standing on the four corners of the earth, holding the four winds of the earth, that the wind should not blow on the earth, nor on the sea, nor on any tree.

2 And I saw another angel ascending from the east, having the seal of the living God: and he cried with a loud voice to the four angels, to whom it was given to hurt the earth and the sea,

3 Saying, Hurt not the earth, neither the sea, nor the trees, till we have sealed the servants of our God in their foreheads.

. . . .

9 After this I beheld, and, lo, a great multitude, which no man could number, of all nations, and kindreds, and people, and tongues, stood before the throne, and before the Lamb, clothed with white robes, and palms in their hands;

10 And cried with a loud voice, saying, Salvation to our God which sitteth upon the throne, and unto the Lamb.

. . . .

13 And one of the elders answered, saying unto me, What are these which are arrayed in white robes? and whence came they?

14 And I said unto him, Sir, thou knowest. And he said to me, These are they which came out of great tribulation, and have washed their robes, and made them white in the blood of the Lamb.

15 Therefore are they before the throne of God, and serve him day and night in his temple: and he that sitteth on the throne shall dwell among them.

16 They shall hunger no more, neither thirst any more; neither shall the sun light on them, nor any heat.

17 For the Lamb which is in the midst of the throne shall feed them, and shall lead them unto living fountains of waters: and God shall wipe away all tears from their eyes.

■ THE LESSON EXPLAINED

The Divine Protection (7:1–8)

Amid universal breakdown, heaven stands secure. No breakdown there. God is in absolute control. And His attention is fixed on earth. He knows He has faithful saints there enduring the horrible last days of earth's existence. "Halt!" He commands. "Wait a minute. Do not open the last seal. No more storms. No more destruction. Go, find My servants. Protect them from all this." Scholars debate soundly who exactly is protected and how this protection relates to all the theories of tribulations, and raptures, and judgments. Space does not allow that discussion here. We can make only one point: when earth's worst times come, God stands in control, and His concern is to protect His people.

The International Procession (7:9-12)

Protected people process in worship. They proclaim the greatness of the One who protects them. God's protected, delivered people forget all differences that separated them on earth. Race, language, politics . . . all differences vanish. God's people unite to praise Him. Even the distinction between heavenly inhabitants and earthly inhabitants vanishes. All join together to praise God. Praise Him, our eternal Protector, forever.

The Perpetual Provision (7:13-17)

God's people are needy people, especially when they endure persecution for their faith. God's people are a crying people. Earth's troubles fill their eyes with tears of pain and sorrow. God's people are redeemed people. Christ's saving blood has made them white as snow. God's people are a homeless people. They are wandering pilgrims looking for the heavenly rest. God's book has a plan. Needs vanish. Food and drink are lavished on them. Persecuted pilgrims find eternal rest in God's mansions. Now they can faithfully serve Him forever. Tears evaporate. God's Redeeming Lamb wipes them all away.

■ TRUTHS TO LIVE BY

You have not seen anything yet. It gets worse. Troubles lead us to despair and doubt. We think no one ever had it so bad. John describes the last days when tribulation covers the earth. The time comes when total disaster, absolute destruction faces the world. The only hope is direct intervention of God. Such days have not yet come. They will.

God protects and provides for His people, even in the worst of times. If God can and wants to call a halt to the final disasters on earth, you can be sure He can take care of you in the minor disasters you face. He will not let His people suffer the final disaster. He has a solution for your problems. He controls the universe. He controls your personal world. Trust Him.

God deserves worship and praise. List what God has done for you. List what He has promised to do for you. List everything you need right now. List everything you will need when you die. How many of those needs can God supply? How many do you think He will supply? Praise Him. Worship. Shout. Sing. Dance. Let the world see how you feel about God. Give Him glory and wisdom and thanksgiving and honor and power. Hallelujah!

■ A VERSE TO REMEMBER

For the Lamb which is in the midst of the throne shall feed them, and shall lead them unto living fountains of waters: and God shall wipe away all tears from their eyes.
—Revelation 7:17

■ DAILY BIBLE READINGS

May 5 — Worship in Spirit and in Truth. John 4:19–26
May 6 — The Lord, Your Keeper. Ps. 121:1–8
May 7 — The Lord, Your Shepherd. Ps. 23:1–6
May 8 — The Lord, Our Comforter. Isa. 25:6–9
May 9 — Jesus, the Good Shepherd. John 10:7–18
May 10 — The Lord, Worthy of Worship. 1 Chron. 16:28–36
May 11 — Jesus Rewards Faithfulness. John 14:15–24

The Victorious Christ

Revelation 19:11–16; 20:11–15

The losers. Somehow they always got my vote. Cleveland Indians: They were my team. I went all the way to St. Louis to see them play the Browns and then to Kansas City to see them play the Royals. While there, Dad and I usually stayed around to see the Yankees play. Of course, I always rooted against the Yankees. They were winners I wanted to lose.

One day it will be different. I am on the winning team now. Often looks different. Do not always see signs of victory. But it is coming. That is sure. I serve the Victorious Christ. When God decides the moment is here, Christ will come with victory in His hands. For once, I know I am on the winning team.

■ THE BIBLE LESSON

REVELATION 19:11–16

11 And I saw heaven opened, and behold a white horse; and he that sat upon him was called Faithful and True, and in righteousness he doth judge and make war.

12 His eyes were as a flame of fire, and on his head were many crowns; and he had a name written, that no man knew, but he himself.

13 And he was clothed with a vesture dipped in blood: and his name is called The Word of God.

14 And the armies which were in heaven followed him upon white horses, clothed in fine linen, white and clean.

15 And out of his mouth goeth a sharp sword, that with it he should smite the nations: and he shall rule them with a rod of iron: and he treadeth the winepress of the fierceness and wrath of Almighty God.

16 And he hath on his vesture and on his thigh a name written, KING OF KINGS, AND LORD OF LORDS.

REVELATION 20:11–15

11 And I saw a great white throne, and him that sat on it, from whose face the earth and the heaven fled away; and there was found no place for them.

12 And I saw the dead, small and great, stand before God; and the books were opened: and another book was opened, which is the book of life: and the dead were judged out of those things which were written in the books, according to their works.

13 And the sea gave up the dead which were in it; and death and hell delivered up the dead which were in them: and they were judged every man according to their works.

14 And death and hell were cast into the lake of fire. This is the second death.

15 And whosoever was not found written in the book of life was cast into the lake of fire.

■ THE LESSON EXPLAINED

The Commander Comes (19:11–16)

Disaster. Tribulation. Warfare. Judgment. Death. Bloodshed. Dragons. These gruesome pictures fill Revelation. They may be the images you take with you from reading the Book. They are not the images John wants to leave with you. They are the preliminaries. They remind you that the troubles you face amount to nothing in light of what is coming. John's final image is Jesus, the Commander-in-Chief of the heavenly armies. He rides out to victory. He represents truth, justice, righteousness. His all-seeing eyes point Him in the directions to go after the enemy. His many crowns show Him to be King over all nations. His secret name shows the mystery about Him that no one can understand and control completely. The blood on His garments shows He has fought and won, the enemies' blood being shed. How can He do this? He is the Eternal Word of God (see John 1).

The pure armies of heaven stand at the Commander's call. Finally, once and for all, divine wrath has reached its limit. One last battle will win the victory once and for all. No more war with Satan. No more unrighteousness. No more persecution of the just. No more suffering and sorrow for God's people. The Commander is winning. The King of Kings and Lord of Lords is here. Victory is ours.

The Judgment Comes (20:11–15)

Victory for us means they lose. What a defeat. Those who oppose Christ must stand before the eternal throne of God. No powers can save them. The devil himself has been defeated (20:10). Everyone who sees God on His throne runs in fear. They cannot escape. They have nowhere to go. Earth's powerful leaders and earth's everyday people all face God together. No one can expect a favor. All stand equal before the holy throne. Judgment is fair. Everything is written down. The evidence is all presented. Everyone is there. No matter how you died, you are raised up to face God's judgment. Every dead person appears. Every living person appears. None escapes. The verdict is passed: Guilty as charged. Sinners deserving to die. Not covered by the blood of the Lamb. Not redeemed by the Calvary sacrifice. They must endure the second death, eternal torment in the lake of fire. The grave cannot protect them. It has been throne into the lake of fire. The devil cannot protect them. He is there, too. The abode of the dead prior to this resurrection and final judgment cannot protect them. It occupies a place in the lake of fire. You must be in Christ's book of life. Otherwise, you face eternal death in the lake of fire. Is your name written down? Why not?

■ TRUTHS TO LIVE BY

Victory is certain. Current appearances deceive. Riches, political power, corruption, evil seem to control our streets, our courts, our political headquarters, our nations. The way to the top is the way of compromise, greed, and evil. Protect yourself or else. That way wins only for a little while. The Commander has saddled His horse. The battle plan is finished. The King of Kings and Lord of Lords is coming. He will win. Are you on His side?

Judgment is certain. Theologians can use all kinds of logic to show that God is too good to send people to eternal hell. Powerful people can enjoy their power and prosperity so much that they ignore all the warning signs. Common people can be so busy making a living and eking out existence that they do not have time to think of eternity No excuses. God is just. Justice demands punishment for sin. God is love. He absorbed sin's punishment in Christ. God is righteous. He does not force any person to accept salvation who does not want it. Life has two possibilities: salvation or judgment. The choice is yours: Victory in Jesus or eternity in hell.

A VERSE TO REMEMBER

And he hath on his vesture and on his thigh a name written, KING OF KINGS, AND LORD OF LORDS.
—Revelation 19:16

DAILY BIBLE READINGS

May 12 — Praise God for His Judgments. Rev. 19:1–5

May 13 — Power Belongs to God. Rev. 19:6–10

May 14 — Punishment of False Prophets. Rev. 19:17–21

May 15 — Christ Will Reign 1,000 Years. Rev. 20:1–6

May 16 — A Kingdom That Cannot Be Shaken. Heb. 12:22–29

May 17 — Our Bodies Will Be Changed. Phil. 3:15–21

May 18 — Jesus Shall Abolish Death. 2 Tim. 1:8–14

A New Heaven and a New Earth

Revelation 21:1–7, 22–27

A house. A real house. Our house. No more apartment living. No more putting up with the noises and bothers of the apartment next door. No more living with the in-laws and trying to abide by all their rules and wishes. We had a house. The joy still vibrates through my body as I remember the feelings. The new adventure thrilled us. In some way it still defines joy and excitement for me. John knew the feeling, many times over. He saw the new house God has ready for all of us who believe. Take a glimpse at your new house through John's inspired eyes.

■ THE BIBLE LESSON

1 And I saw a new heaven and a new earth: for the first heaven and the first earth were passed away; and there was no more sea.

2 And I John saw the holy city, new Jerusalem, coming down from God out of heaven, prepared as a bride adorned for her husband.

3 And I heard a great voice out of heaven saying, Behold, the tabernacle of God is with men, and he will dwell with them, and they shall be his people, and God himself shall be with them, and be their God.

4 And God shall wipe away all tears from their eyes; and there shall be no more death, neither sorrow, nor crying, neither shall there be any more pain: for the former things are passed away.

5 And he that sat upon the throne said, Behold, I make all things new. And he said unto me, Write: for these words are true and faithful.

6 And he said unto me, It is done. I am Alpha and Omega, the beginning and the end. I will give unto him that is athirst of the fountain of the water of life freely.

7 He that overcometh shall inherit all things; and I will be his God, and he shall be my son.

....

22 And I saw no temple therein: for the Lord God Almighty and the Lamb are the temple of it.

23 And the city had no need of the sun, neither of the moon, to shine in it: for the glory of God did lighten it, and the Lamb is the light thereof.

24 And the nations of them which are saved shall walk in the light of it: and the kings of the earth do bring their glory and honour into it.

25 And the gates of it shall not be shut at all by day: for there shall be no night there.

26 And they shall bring the glory and honour of the nations into it.

27 And there shall in no wise enter into it any thing that defileth, neither whatsoever worketh abomination, or maketh a lie: but they which are written in the Lamb's book of life.

■ THE LESSON EXPLAINED

Eternal Presence (21:1-4)

Nothing that exists is good enough for eternity. God makes everything all over again for His people to enjoy. The raging fearful sea, the home of sea monsters and wrecked ships and human fears, vanishes. Its purposes have passed. Even the holy city Jerusalem cannot remain. A new Jerusalem replaces it. Eternity is not a life of isolated bliss. It is a life of community, people living in a city. What is different? God is there. Jerusalem no longer just represents God's dwelling place with His people. Now Jerusalem is the Holy City, holy and pure enough for God to live there with His redeemed, holy, pure people. God's presence means all is well. No tears, no sorrow, no suffering, no death, no sad memories. Eternal life in the eternal Presence.

Eternal Family (21:5-8)

Sounds like a dream, too good to be true? John assures us it is no dream. God Himself dictated the promise. He is

Truth. He cannot lie. Who will live there? Those who overcome (note the letters to the churches in chapters 2–3). They will form the new family: God is Parent. We are children. Who will be missing? Those who are in the lake of fire, suffering the second death, those who refused to obey and experience God on earth. If you do not want God's presence here, you surely could not stand it for eternity. Your choice?

Eternal Worship (21:9–22)

What is this new home like? It is a house fit for the Husband, the Redeeming Lamb, Jesus Himself. It is equipped to house God's glory. It is made of the perfect building materials to give the most glorious view possible. It is a city built on the faith of the original twelve apostles. The city is large enough to accommodate all its holy citizens and perfectly symmetrical to please the most demanding architect.

Something's missing. Jerusalem does not have a temple. No need for a temple in this Jerusalem. The veil has been broken. The temple cannot be the hiding place, keeping people from intruding on the Holy One. He has made the people holy. Yes, Father and Son walk the streets of the city with the people. He is present face to face. Life is a constant worship experience. You do not have to travel anywhere to worship. God is right with you.

Eternal Glory (21:23–27)

Look at this new world. No sun. No moon. No stars. What's up? God's shining glory provides all the light needed. Earthly glory fades. The kings now come to God to honor His glory. Their power and magnificence mean nothing in that light. No fears. You can come and go any time you want. Night never comes. Darkness never appears. God's glory shines forever. Nothing can detract from that glory, for all sin is destroyed. All lies are vanquished. Only the holy ones, redeemed by the blood of the Lamb and written in His book of life, inhabit His city.

■ TRUTHS TO LIVE BY

Heaven is beyond any experience you ever had. Heaven is new, different, perfect. John can only paint word pictures trying to make you want to be part of it. All earthly treasure, all earthly possessions, all earthly desires fail to measure up. They do not belong in heaven. They are not rich enough, pure enough, beautiful enough, perfect enough. Heaven is God's new creation with no sin to blemish it. Heaven meets all the standards for God's permanent place of residence. Do you want to live there?

Heaven is a community. Heaven is the perfect family affair. Everyone is an equal child of the heavenly Father. He cares for all needs, so that negative experiences never occur. Learn to live happily with the people of God now, for you will spend eternity with them.

Heaven centers on the presence of God. Heaven is not the sum total of all the riches and frills you have ever wanted to possess. Heaven does not transfer you from want to wealth, from rags to riches, from fantasy to fantastic. Heaven places you in the everlasting presence of God and lets you enjoy worshiping and serving Him forever. Worship practice starts here and is perfected there.

■ A VERSE TO REMEMBER

And I saw a new heaven and a new earth: for the first heaven and the first earth were passed away; and there was no more sea.—Revelation 21:1

■ DAILY BIBLE READINGS

May 19 — The New Jerusalem. Rev. 21:9–14
May 20 — The City's Measurements. Rev. 21:15–21
May 21 — The City's Blessings. Rev. 22:1–5
May 22 — A Trustworthy Book. Rev. 22:6–14
May 23 — A Certain Return. Rev. 22:16–20
May 24 — Zion's Future Glory. Isa. 60:1–5
May 25 — Grow in Knowledge As You Wait. 2 Pet. 3:8–18

Christ's Servant Sets an Example

1 Timothy 4:6–16

What do you teach a preacher? Ten years spent teaching in seminary made me ponder the question often. Now in the publishing ministry I view it from a different perspective. The answer remains elusive. How do you take a person God has gifted and called to ministry and provide training that will help that person in the local church? Paul set the example as he wrote to Timothy and Titus. We will follow him for five weeks as he helps young preachers learn how to do their job. He began with a "to do" list and a "not to do" list.

■ THE BIBLE LESSON

6 If thou put the brethren in remembrance of these things, thou shalt be a good minister of Jesus Christ, nourished up in the words of faith and of good doctrine, whereunto thou hast attained.

7 But refuse profane and old wives' fables, and exercise thyself rather unto godliness.

8 For bodily exercise profiteth little: but godliness is profitable unto all things, having promise of the life that now is, and of that which is to come.

9 This is a faithful saying and worthy of all acceptation.

10 For therefore we both labour and suffer reproach, because we trust in the living God, who is the Saviour of all men, specially of those that believe.

11 These things command and teach.

12 Let no man despise thy youth; but be thou an example of the believers, in word, in conversation, in charity, in spirit, in faith, in purity.

13 Till I come, give attendance to reading, to exhortation, to doctrine.

14 Neglect not the gift that is in thee, which was given thee by prophecy, with the laying on of the hands of the presbytery.

15 Meditate upon these things; give thyself wholly to them; that thy profiting may appear to all.

16 Take heed unto thyself, and unto the doctrine; continue in them: for in doing this thou shalt both save thyself, and them that hear thee.

■ THE LESSON EXPLAINED

Things Not to Teach (4:6–10)

People teach all kinds of things in the name of Christianity. They have done it for a long time. Paul listed several of these false teachings for Timothy (vv. 1–3). Timothy, the first thing to learn is not to teach such things. Learn to distinguish what is right and what is wrong. Do not listen to every preacher who comes along and use his sermons because they sound good or because people seem to like them. Know the truth. Learn the Word for yourself. Know the doctrine the Word teaches. Then you can determine what to accept and what to reject from the teaching of other people. Some things will be so obviously wrong you can ignore them. They are just old wives' tales, unworthy of being heard or repeated. Take the time you would spend listening to get a spiritual tune up. Train yourself to act as God wants you to act. How do you do this? Not by punishing your body, beating it into shape, refusing to feed it, trying to show the world how religious you are. Godliness comes by training yourself in the positive things of God just as an athlete trains. Participate in spiritual disciplines to increase your spirituality. Then you have life here and hereafter. This is not easy. It takes work and suffering. Others will laugh at you. Why do it, then? Because God has saved you and told you spiritual discipline is good for you. Trust what He says, not what humans laugh at.

Things to Teach (4:11–16)

Timothy, you are a minister called to teach and train others. This is hard for you at times. People say you are too young and inexperienced. You have only one way to prove them wrong. Live the mature Christian life. The words you say . . . the activities you participate in . . . the ways you help other people and show Christ's love to them . . . the spirit and attitude you show in all you do and say every day . . . the faith you witness to and demonstrate . . . the moral purity of your life—all these must be just what God has commanded. If people are to trust you as a minister, they must find reason to in the life you live. You are their example of Christ.

I know you want to be near me and learn from me. I cannot come now. What can you do? Read and study the Scriptures. Encourage and train the people. Learn and teach the truth. God gave you gifts for ministry. The church elders or pastors witnessed to these as they laid on hands and ordained you to the ministry. Now look back over the things which I have said. Think about them. Meditate on them. Practice them. Make them part of your life all day every day. Everyone will see. Then the church members will respect you and follow your leadership. Then both you and your church will remain on the course dictated by salvation.

■ TRUTHS TO LIVE BY

Preachers should know the difference between true and false doctrine. The pastor has the responsibility to study Scripture and pray intensely so that false doctrine automatically registers as false when it is heard. No matter how popular a doctrine may become with preachers and churches, no pastor has an excuse for preaching doctrine that does not agree with the Bible.

Preachers should practice spiritual disciplines. Prayer, Bible study, meditation, intercession, and moral living are minimum expectations God has of the preacher. No excuse suffices to neglect these. They are the foundation of ministry. No other ministry can be done well by a pastor unprepared spiritually.

Preachers gain leadership through spiritual living. Following Paul's "to do" and "not to do" lists changes the life of the minister. The minister can never demand pastoral authority from the congregation. The minister can earn it through personal spiritual growth and daily obedience in the experience of the presence of Christ.

■ VERSES TO REMEMBER

But refuse profane and old wives' fables, and exercise thyself rather unto godliness. For bodily exercise profiteth little: but godliness is profitable unto all things, having promise of the life that now is, and of that which is to come.
—1 Timothy 4:7–8

■ DAILY BIBLE READINGS

May 26 — Set a Good Example. Ps. 37:1–11
May 27 — Be Wise. Prov. 23:15–25
May 28 — Be Trustworthy. 1 Cor. 4:1–5
May 29 — Be Humble. 1 Cor. 4:6–13
May 30 — Be Faithful As God Is Faithful. 1 Thess. 4:1–5
May 31 — Beware of False Doctrines. 1 Tim. 4:1–5
June 1 — Preach Christ Crucified. 1 Cor. 1:10–25

Christ's Servant Teaches Godliness

1 Timothy 6:2b–21

She was the preacher's wife. Her father had all the money in the world, it seemed. I was a missionary. I had no money, it seemed. They traveled everywhere. Did anything they wanted. Bought everything in sight. Even lived any way they wanted. Money could buy them out of any trouble they got into. Why couldn't I have just a little of what they had? Surely God did not want me to see so many things I would like to have and so many people I would like to help and not be able. The rich preacher and his wife could not stay together. Nor could they find happiness. Paul showed us why long ago. I am still trying to learn and live Paul's lessons. Are you?

■ THE BIBLE LESSON

2 These things teach and exhort.

3 If any man teach otherwise, and consent not to wholesome words, even the words of our Lord Jesus Christ, and to the doctrine which is according to godliness;

4 He is proud, knowing nothing, but doting about questions and strifes of words, whereof cometh envy, strife, railings, evil surmisings,

5 Perverse disputings of men of corrupt minds, and destitute of the truth, supposing that gain is godliness: from such withdraw thyself.

6 But godliness with contentment is great gain.

7 For we brought nothing into this world, and it is certain we can carry nothing out.

8 And having food and raiment let us be therewith content.

9 But they that will be rich fall into temptation and a snare, and into many foolish and hurtful lusts, which drown men in destruction and perdition.

10 For the love of money is the root of all evil: which while some coveted after, they have erred from the faith, and pierced themselves through with many sorrows.

11 But thou, O man of God, flee these things; and follow after righteousness, godliness, faith, love, patience, meekness.

12 Fight the good fight of faith, lay hold on eternal life, whereunto thou art also called, and hast professed a good profession before many witnesses.

13 I give thee charge in the sight of God, who quickeneth all things, and before Christ Jesus, who before Pontius Pilate witnessed a good confession;

14 That thou keep this commandment without spot, unrebukeable, until the appearing of our LORD JESUS CHRIST:

15 Which in his times he shall shew, who is the blessed and only Potentate, the King of kings, and LORD of lords;

16 Who only hath immortality, dwelling in the light which no man can approach unto; whom no man hath seen, nor can see: to whom be honour and power everlasting. Amen.

17 Charge them that are rich in this world, that they be not highminded, nor trust in uncertain riches, but in the living God, who giveth us richly all things to enjoy;

18 That they do good, that they be rich in good works, ready to distribute, willing to communicate;

19 Laying up in store for themselves a good foundation against the time to come, that they may lay hold on eternal life.

20 O Timothy, keep that which is committed to thy trust, avoiding profane and vain babblings, and oppositions of science falsely so called:

21 Which some professing have erred concerning the faith. Grace be with thee. Amen.

THE LESSON EXPLAINED

False Teaching (6:2-5)

Where does false teaching lead? Why worry about it? Paul knew. False doctrine leads to false living. False teachers become proud. They say a lot but finally show they really know nothing. They make a name for themselves by always getting into debates and arguments with other people. This leads to envy, fighting, calling other people names, making up evil stories about other people. The final result: evil men fighting and arguing all the time without one shred of truth. Greed and money become the goals of life. The people of God have one choice: get away from these people.

False Living (6:6-10)

Is it better to be right or to be content? Paul says contentment is the goal. Godly living is the way. You owned nothing when you were born and were totally content as long as Mom and Dad gave you food and kept you warmly clothed. Why want more now? Wealth only brings temptations to depend on yourself and indulge in evil desires. The result is ruin, destruction, judgment. To love money is to grow a life on the wrong root. Life built around money is life devoted to evil. It remains nearly impossible for a rich person to enter the kingdom of heaven. Be content with godliness.

True Living (6:11-16)

Money paves the road to evil and godlessness. Faith paves the road to righteousness, godliness, love, patience, trust, meekness. Such a life does not come easily. It is a continuous fight against temptations of false living. It makes eternal life the goal rather than money. Why choose eternal life over money? Look at Jesus. He gave His life to show you the importance of salvation and eternal life. Eternal life is so valuable it cost God His only Son. Can't you pay the price of godliness until Jesus returns? Then you can live with Jesus, who is God Himself.

True Teaching (6:17-21)

Must I choose riches or eternal life? Most of the time, that is true. What if I am rich now? No hope for me? It depends on your attitude. Does money make you proud? Do you think you can get anything you need with your money? Do you not depend on God for anything? Do you share your wealth with those in need? Do you minister in Christ's name to other people? Or does money isolate you from other people, making you think you are better than they are? Are you more concerned about protecting your money or making sure you have eternal life?

Timothy, you have a bank account in heaven. Protect it. Don't let these false teachers and teachings take it away from you. Don't substitute money for God. Don't let their talk so impress you that you forget the truth you learned from God. Hold and live the true. Reject the false.

TRUTHS TO LIVE BY

Money is attractive. Financial security and material possessions allure most of us. Few are not tempted to give up a little faith to have a lot of money.

Money is dangerous. Money becomes the goal of living. Money gives a sense of security that makes us depend on it and not on God. Money can purchase protection from the worries and frustrations that most people endure. Money becomes god before we know it.

Money is temporary. If you keep your money in life, you lose it in death. Then what do you have? Money cannot purchase eternal security. You need a deposit of faith in heaven's bank. Do you have it?

VERSES TO REMEMBER

But thou, O man of God, flee these things; and follow after righteousness, godliness, faith, love, patience, meekness. Fight the good fight of faith, lay hold on eternal life, whereunto thou art also called, and hast professed a good profession before many witnesses.—1 Timothy 6:11–12

■ DAILY BIBLE READINGS

June 2—Keep Above Reproach. 1 Tim. 6:13–21
June 3—Keep Yourself Pure. 1 Tim. 5:17–24
June 4—Approve That Which Is Good. Phil. 1:3–11
June 5—Do Not Love the World. 1 John 2:12–17
June 6—Accept the Love of Christ. Eph. 3:14–21
June 7—Follow Christ's Example. Luke 12:13–21
June 8—God's Divine Power Grants Godliness. 2 Pet. 1:3–11

Christ's Servant Endures Suffering

2 Timothy 2:1–13

His name escapes me. His face will always linger in my mind. He pointed straight ahead. "See those trees across the valley? Look closely through the trees. See the turrets of the tanks? Our church here in eastern Poland is the first stop for the Russian invasion. The sad thing is the senior citizens' home our church sponsors. It will be the first casualty of war." Fortunately, the tanks did not come, but that sainted pastor showed me the meaning of suffering for Jesus as he led worship each Sunday staring down the gun barrels.

■ THE BIBLE LESSON

1 Thou therefore, my son, be strong in the grace that is in Christ Jesus.

2 And the things that thou hast heard of me among many witnesses, the same commit thou to faithful men, who shall be able to teach others also.

3 Thou therefore endure hardness, as a good soldier of Jesus Christ.

4 No man that warreth entangleth himself with the affairs of this life; that he may please him who hath chosen him to be a soldier.

5 And if a man also strive for masteries, yet is he not crowned, except he strive lawfully.

6 The husbandman that laboureth must be first partaker of the fruits.

7 Consider what I say; and the Lord give thee understanding in all things.

8 Remember that Jesus Christ of the seed of David was raised from the dead according to my gospel:

9 Wherein I suffer trouble, as an evildoer, even unto bonds; but the word of God is not bound.

10 Therefore I endure all things for the elect's sakes, that they may also obtain the salvation which is in Christ Jesus with eternal glory.

11 It is a faithful saying: For if we be dead with him, we shall also live with him:

12 If we suffer, we shall also reign with him: if we deny him, he also will deny us:

13 If we believe not, yet he abideth faithful: he cannot deny himself.

■ THE LESSON EXPLAINED

Strong in Grace (2:1-3)

My beloved son in the ministry. Let me share some secrets you need as you lead God's people. You have to be strong. Ministry is no place for weaklings. Do you know where you get strength? Certainly not from yourself. You have to depend on God's grace that He showed to us in Jesus. Grace brings you more than salvation. Grace brings you God's power to operate in ministry day by day. Depend on it. What do you do with the strength God gives you? You share it. You are not a one-person show. Ministry requires the entire church. Take what God gives you and give it to others. Let me share with you in sharing God's good news. Know that God gives you strength for a purpose. You are fighting a war. Satan's army is huge. Fighting him is hard work. Life on God's battlefield is not easy. You will have to have God's strength to endure. Fight the good fight.

Striving for Victory (2:4-7)

The fight requires concentration. You cannot try to succeed in the world and fight God's battle at the same time. You know the one Commanding Officer. Concentrate on His orders. Forget all else. You are like a long distance runner. You must discipline yourself and be ready for the long haul.

You must know the rules for the race and obey them. Then you will get a prize. Just so in God's battle game of life. You must understand God's rules for living, discipline yourself in godliness, and wait for the prize until the race is run. Be assured. God knows who is on His side. He knows you deserve the fruits of victory just like a farmer deserves the first choice of food from his crop. Don't just listen to what I say and forget. Think about it. Meditate on it. Ask God to help you know what you must know to be a minister.

Suffering for the Church (2:8–13)

Above all think about one thing. Think about Jesus Christ and what He has done for you. He died, and God raised Him from the dead. Therefore, you have hope for victory. Never forget that. How in the world can I say such things? You know my condition. I am in prison, in chains, probably facing death. That does not bother me. No one can put God's Word in chains. Learn it. Teach it. Preach it. Live by it. What happens to you, how much you suffer, matters not. What matters is that God's people hear His Word and respond to it. They can hear it only as you share it. Then they will have eternal salvation. That is reason enough to forget your suffering and remember to share. You may die for Christ. So what. He promised you would live with Him and rule in His kingdom. The other choice? Deny Him. The result: no salvation, no eternal life, no life in His kingdom. He will be faithful. Will you?

■ TRUTHS TO LIVE BY

God's grace is the only source of strength. Strength you gain from any other source will prove too weak in the time of crisis. Depending on God's love and grace assures you of the physical and spiritual power to carry out the mission He gives you.

Christ's resurrection is your assurance. Because Jesus rose from the dead, you know the final victory is yours and life's highest prize is yours. You will live eternally with Him. The choice is yours: faithful to death or deny Him and His eternal life.

Christ's lifestyle for you involves suffering. To minister for Christ, you must work hard, discipline yourself daily, and endure the suffering caused by the world's attacks. If you suffer nothing for your faith, you need to check how much faith you have.

■ A VERSE TO REMEMBER

Thou therefore endure hardness, as a good soldier of Jesus Christ.—2 Timothy 2:3

■ DAILY BIBLE READINGS

June 9— Jesus' Suffering Foretold. Luke 9:18–27
June 10— Christ Suffered for Us. 1 Pet. 2:18–25
June 11— Suffer for Righteousness. 1 Pet. 3:13–25
June 12— Be Proud to Suffer for Christ. 1 Pet. 4:12–19
June 13— Rejoice in Suffering. Col. 1:24–29
June 14— Suffering Produces Character. Rom. 5:1–10
June 15— God Is Our Comforter. 2 Cor. 1:3–11

Christ's Servant Teaches Faithfulness

2 Timothy 4:1–8

Tommy Lee. Ask anyone around the organization about Tommy Lee and they will have an interesting story. He worked at the organization for who knows how many years, longer than any one else around. I guess he must have had a title and a job description, but I do not know what it was. He just did everything that needed to be done to get the materials published and keep the employees happy. His smiling face epitomizes faithfulness for me.

■ THE BIBLE LESSON

1 I charge thee therefore before God, and the Lord Jesus Christ, who shall judge the quick and the dead at his appearing and his kingdom;

2 Preach the word; be instant in season, out of season; reprove, rebuke, exhort with all longsuffering and doctrine.

3 For the time will come when they will not endure sound doctrine; but after their own lusts shall they heap to themselves teachers, having itching ears;

4 And they shall turn away their ears from the truth, and shall be turned unto fables.

5 But watch thou in all things, endure afflictions, do the work of an evangelist, make full proof of thy ministry.

6 For I am now ready to be offered, and the time of my departure is at hand.

7 I have fought a good fight, I have finished my course, I have kept the faith:

8 Henceforth there is laid up for me a crown of righteousness, which the Lord, the righteous judge, shall give me at that day: and not to me only, but unto all them also that love his appearing.

THE LESSON EXPLAINED

Immoral Times Require Faithfulness (4:1–4)

Timothy, my son and successor in ministry. You have heard all I had to say. Now, let me summarize all that I have tried to tell you in one final charge. God and His Son Jesus are my witnesses as you promise to be faithful to the ministry They and I leave with you. You know you will face Jesus at the Last Judgment, so make no promises you do not mean to keep. You are a preacher. That means preach the gospel. Preach its whole truth. Apply it to the situation as the situation demands. At every opportunity, to many people or to few, preach the Word. Tell people when they are not obeying the gospel. Encourage the faithful when they are blue. Do so with loving patience and with true doctrine. This is urgent, for you will not always have the opportunity. The time comes when people will be so dedicated to evil that they will not even listen to the gospel. They want preachers who say what they want to hear and give them gossip they can pass on to others. Preach the Word while you can.

Personal Testimony Encourages Faithfulness (4:5–8)

Timothy, such immorality means you must be alert. You must know truth when you hear it. You must know falsehood when you hear it. They will persecute you like they did me. All you can do is endure it. Keep telling them about Jesus. Minister to people wherever you see need. Represent Jesus. Show His love to all people. You have to take up the work, for you will not have me with you much longer. I am in prison and about to surrender my life for the sake of the gospel. I have nothing to be ashamed of. I can testify from personal experience: faithfulness to the gospel is worth everything you have to suffer. God will reward me in heaven. That is all I want. He will do the same for you and for all that love Him. So be faithful every day, even if you have to die for Him. The reward is worth the pain.

TRUTHS TO LIVE BY

Live the present with a view to the future. Concern for immediate reward may lead you to deny Christ and live in sin. Looking only at the present may take your eyes off Jesus. Live every moment with your eyes on the reward God has waiting for you in heaven. That makes anything that happens in the present endurable.

Live the Word in every situation. Many teachers will offer tempting words that lead to immediate "pleasure." They will say what you want to hear. The only way to stay on God's pathway of life is to stay in His Word. Find something in His Word that helps you react to each situation. Live out His Word in front of every person you meet. That is the way you can do the work of an evangelist.

Live with suffering as Paul and Jesus did. The world's way is to compare your life to modern heroes and modern success stories. You may feel God slights you because you do not get what someone else has. God's way is to look at the Cross. See what Jesus did, what He gave up, what He suffered, how He showed love, how He followed the path God opened for Him. In that light, how much have you suffered? Are you willing to be faithful?

VERSES TO REMEMBER

I charge thee therefore before God, and the Lord Jesus Christ, who shall judge the quick and the dead at his appearing and his kingdom; Preach the word; be instant in season, out of season; reprove, rebuke, exhort with all longsuffering and doctrine.—2 Timothy 4:1–2

DAILY BIBLE READINGS

June 16 — The Lord's Laws Are Forever. Ps. 119:89–96
June 17 — Praise the Lord for His Faithfulness. Ps. 32:19–24
June 18 — Faithful in Spite of Trials. 2 Tim. 4:9–18
June 19 — Be As Faithful As God's Child. Rom. 8:12–20
June 20 — Be Faithful over Small Things. Luke 16:10–11
June 21 — The Lord Requires Faithfulness. Deut. 10:12–20
June 22 — Faithfulness Will Be Rewarded. 1 Pet. 5:1–11

Christ's Servant Encourages Community

Titus 3:1–11

A local pastor stirred up our community recently announcing he might run for mayor. Was he crossing the line of separation between church and state? Or was he following Paul's advice to young pastor Titus to be a good citizen? The debate will continue a long time in this community. You and your church need to decide what the Bible says about your citizenship in the community.

■ THE BIBLE LESSON

1 Put them in mind to be subject to principalities and powers, to obey magistrates, to be ready to every good work,

2 To speak evil of no man, to be no brawlers, but gentle, shewing all meekness unto all men.

3 For we ourselves also were sometimes foolish, disobedient, deceived, serving divers lusts and pleasures, living in malice and envy, hateful, and hating one another.

4 But after that the kindness and love of God our Saviour toward man appeared,

5 Not by works of righteousness which we have done, but according to his mercy he saved us, by the washing of regeneration, and renewing of the Holy Ghost;

6 Which he shed on us abundantly through Jesus Christ our Saviour;

7 That being justified by his grace, we should be made heirs according to the hope of eternal life.

8 This is a faithful saying, and these things I will that thou affirm constantly, that they which have believed in God might be careful to maintain good works. These things are good and profitable unto men.

9 But avoid foolish questions, and genealogies, and contentions, and strivings about the law; for they are unprofitable and vain.

10 A man that is an heretic after the first and second admonition reject;

11 Knowing that he that is such is subverted, and sinneth, being condemned of himself.

THE LESSON EXPLAINED

Live Up to Community Expectations (3:1-2)

Titus, you are in some trouble. I left you in Crete to lead the churches there and install local leadership in the churches. You have found heretics there who flood the people with false teachings. I need to give you a few other reminders that will help. Your people must quit thinking Christ's kingdom separates them from the world. They are still citizens of the government. Christ gives them no right to ignore what the government says. We witness to the pagan world best when we are better citizens than they are. Do everything good for the community that you can possibly do. Kingdom citizenship never gives you reason to be proud, to set yourself up as better than someone else, or to say ugly things about another person. Meek humility is the attitude Christ showed. We must show it to the world.

Live Up to Christ's Love (3:3-8)

How can they so quickly forget? They have no reason for pride. Remember what they used to be. Were they any better than the people they now look down on? They had lust and hatred just like unbelievers still do. What happened? Did they suddenly get better? No, suddenly Jesus showed them God's love and kindness and took charge of their lives. He washed us with His blood and took charge of our emotions, our attitudes, and our actions by placing the Holy Spirit in us. He gave us hope of eternal life with Christ. How can you experience all Jesus in His grace did for you and then look down with contempt on another person created in God's image? Don't look down on people. Look up to Christ's love and try to live up to it.

Live Without Willful Sinners (3:9–11)

Titus, you have a serious problem in the church. People want to argue about meaningless things, things they can find no right answer to. You and I both know some people in your church have beliefs that separate them from Jesus Christ. They are heretics. They point to a way of salvation that adds something to the grace of God and repentance and faith by sinners. They attempt to divide the church. You have warned them once. Give them a second and final warning. Then put them out of the church until they are willing to be good church members, not divisive ones.

Christ's church must present a unified front to the community and teach salvation through Jesus Christ and His cross with nothing added.

■ TRUTHS TO LIVE BY

You have two citizenships. Believing in Christ, you join His kingdom. You are under His absolute rule for your life. You have always belonged to an earthly nation. You do not give up citizenship there to join Christ's kingdom. Christ's rule leads you to be the best citizen the earthly nation has. You are a good citizen in two kingdoms.

You have no reason to think you are better than anyone else. One thing makes you different from other people. You have experienced Jesus' salvation in grace. They have not. Your responsibility is to be such a good citizen according to their definition of citizenship that they will want to know how and why you do it.

You have responsibility to keep the church membership rolls clean. The church must present a unified front to the world. People who try to divide you need to leave. Show them the problem they create. Give them a second chance.

If they still refuse to be good church members, then treat them the way they are acting—as non-believers.

■ A VERSE TO REMEMBER

This is a faithful saying, and these things I will that thou affirm constantly, that they which have believed in God might be careful to maintain good works. These things are good and profitable unto men.—Titus 3:8

■ DAILY BIBLE READINGS

June 23— Avoid Disputes. 2 Tim. 2:14–19
June 24— Support Faithful Workers. Phil. 4:10–20
June 25— Teach Sound Doctrines. Titus 2:1–8
June 26— Teach with Authority. Titus 2:9–19
June 27— Forgive One Another. 2 Cor. 2:5–11
June 28— All Are Guilty under the Law. Rom. 3:9–20
June 29— All Are Justified by God's Grace. Rom. 3:21–31

Jesus Is God's Son

Hebrews 1:1–5; 3:1–6

"Keep on keeping on? Why should I? I've tried the church long enough. It just does not deliver on its promises. Sounds too good to be true, and it is!" Such thoughts ever cross your mind? A group of first-century Jews certainly pondered them. The mysterious, anonymous writer of Hebrews counter-attacked. He had one good reason for keeping on in the faith of Christianity: the person of Jesus Christ. Unequaled in all history, He did what no other religion or person has ever accomplished. Knowing Him is worth everything you ever suffered and more. Why? Read on.

■ THE BIBLE LESSON

1 God, who at sundry times and in divers manners spake in time past unto the fathers by the prophets,

2 Hath in these last days spoken unto us by his Son, whom he hath appointed heir of all things, by whom also he made the worlds;

3 Who being the brightness of his glory, and the express image of his person, and upholding all things by the word of his power, when he had by himself purged our sins, sat down on the right hand of the Majesty on high;

4 Being made so much better than the angels, as he hath by inheritance obtained a more excellent name than they.

5 For unto which of the angels said he at any time, Thou art my Son, this day have I begotten thee? And again, I will be to him a Father, and he shall be to me a Son?

....

1 Wherefore, holy brethren, partakers of the heavenly calling, consider the Apostle and High Priest of our profession, Christ Jesus;

2 Who was faithful to him that appointed him, as also Moses was faithful in all his house.

3 For this man was counted worthy of more glory than Moses, inasmuch as he who hath builded the house hath more honour than the house.

4 For every house is builded by some man; but he that built all things is God.

5 And Moses verily was faithful in all his house, as a servant, for a testimony of those things which were to be spoken after;

6 But Christ as a son over his own house; whose house are we, if we hold fast the confidence and the rejoicing of the hope firm unto the end.

THE LESSON EXPLAINED

Jesus Shows You What God Is Like (1:1–3)

No polite openings. No introductions of who writes and who receives. Just the startling word: God. So Hebrews opens, letting you know immediately its subject. Thirteen chapters about God. Can you think of any more important subject? But how can you know anything about God? Has anyone ever really seen Him? You define Him as Invisible, so how can you talk about Him? Very easily. We do not have to rely just on what other people said and talked about. We have seen Jesus. Jesus was part of creation. He sustains and maintains everything created. Jesus is God's Son; the One who owns everything. He is the One who died to take care of our sin problem. Jesus is exactly like God. When you see Jesus, you see God. So we can talk about God, because we saw Jesus.

Jesus Is Superior to All Other Creatures (1:4–5)

Angels! Everyone likes to talk about angels. They are so pretty to look at. They make you feel good. You think one of them might even be guarding you and protecting you. Forget about angels! Jesus is so much better. He is the Son of

God. Let that sink in. He and He alone stands to inherit everything the Father has. He alone has all the power and authority the Father has. He has a better, stronger reputation than anyone you can name. He is everything we expected from the Messiah we read about in the Old Testament (see Ps. 2:7; 89:26).

Jesus Shows Us How to Be Faithful (3:1–6)

Let's have a family talk for a minute. We need to know what this Jesus thing means day by day for our lives. You have accepted God's call and joined His family. You know who Jesus is. He is the One God sent to us. He is the One we profess as our High Priest, Who took care of our sin problem once and for all. He faithfully did everything God asked Him to do. You have always revered Moses and his great faithfulness to God under trying circumstances. Jesus is better than Moses. Moses was simply a servant. Jesus is the Son who owns and controls everything. But what does all this have to do with living today? Jesus shows us what faithfulness is. Faithfulness is staying confident that Jesus will do what He promised. Faithfulness is staying full of joy no matter what happens. How can we do this? Because Jesus has given us something to look forward to. He has given us hope. No one else has. Stay faithful to Jesus.

■ TRUTHS TO LIVE BY

Jesus has provided your salvation. Never forget this. Repeat it every day. Let this truth give you courage, hope, faithfulness, and joy. Salvation is complete. Jesus did everything. Now hold on to Jesus, and forget anything that would lead you away from Jesus.

Jesus is God and has God's power and authority. Life can become a power search, an authority struggle. You want to be "one up" on everybody else. Life does not have to be a power search. Jesus can give you a power surge. Trust Him so you can quit fighting everyone else.

Jesus shows you how to live in faith. Jesus obeyed everything God said, even leaving heaven to die on earth. Will you imitate Him? Listen to God. Do what God says. Listen to no one else.

■ VERSES TO REMEMBER

Wherefore, holy brethren, partakers of the heavenly calling, consider the Apostle and High Priest of our profession, Christ Jesus; Who was faithful to him that appointed him, as also Moses was faithful in all his house.—Hebrews 3:1–2

■ DAILY BIBLE READINGS

June 30— Christ Is Eternal. Heb. 1:7–14
July 1 — Christ Is over All. Eph. 1:15–23
July 2 — Christ Came from God. John 8:34–42
July 3 — Christ, Son and Heir of God. Gal. 4:1–7
July 4 — To Know Christ Is to Know God. John 14:1–7
July 5 — Confess Christ as God's Son. John 4:13–21
July 6 — Christ Came to Do God's Will. John 6:35–40

Jesus Is Savior

Hebrews 2:5–11, 14–18

Someone saved me. I do not know who. They found me lying in a ditch, car wrecked, head cut open almost ear to ear, bleeding slowly to death. They stopped, called the ambulance, got the doctors, saved my life. But I never discovered who saved me. I have another salvation experience. I know who saved me then. I know that salvation still holds, because Jesus is my Savior. I hope He is yours.

■ THE BIBLE LESSON

5 For unto the angels hath he not put in subjection the world to come, whereof we speak.

6 But one in a certain place testified, saying, What is man, that thou art mindful of him? or the son of man, that thou visitest him?

7 Thou madest him a little lower than the angels; thou crownedst him with glory and honour, and didst set him over the works of thy hands:

8 Thou hast put all things in subjection under his feet. For in that he put all in subjection under him, he left nothing that is not put under him. But now we see not yet all things put under him.

9 But we see Jesus, who was made a little lower than the angels for the suffering of death, crowned with glory and honour; that he by the grace of God should taste death for every man.

10 For it became him, for whom are all things, and by whom are all things, in bringing many sons unto glory, to make the captain of their salvation perfect through sufferings.

11 For both he that sanctifieth and they who are sanctified are all of one: for which cause he is not ashamed to call them brethren,

14 Forasmuch then as the children are partakers of flesh and blood, he also himself likewise took part of the same; that through death he might destroy him that had the power of death, that is, the devil;

15 And deliver them who through fear of death were all their lifetime subject to bondage.

16 For verily he took not on him the nature of angels; but he took on him the seed of Abraham.

17 Wherefore in all things it behoved him to be made like unto his brethren, that he might be a merciful and faithful high priest in things pertaining to God, to make reconciliation for the sins of the people.

18 For in that he himself hath suffered being tempted, he is able to succour them that are tempted.

■ THE LESSON EXPLAINED

The Power of People (5:5–8)

Who was important enough for God to work a plan of salvation for them? You and I, human beings, people. Look what God did for us. He created an entire universe for us to inhabit. Why? Because we deserved it? Of course not! Because in His wisdom and love He chose to. Psalm 8:4 shows us how important we are. We rank high in His hierarchy, just below the angels. Even the angels did not gain control of the world. We did. God chose to give us power over all He created, to keep it and protect it (Gen. 1:26–28). Yes, God trusted us to be in charge of all He created. But it has not happened that way. We are out of control, not in control. That is just what the Bible says. We sinned and did not exercise control like God wanted. So look what He did.

The Power of Suffering (5:9–13)

God took His own Son in heaven and sent Him down to become lower than the angels, a human just like we are. Jesus had one mission: suffer for our sins. Mission accomplished. Result: Jesus gains a crown more splendid than anything the high priest ever wore (see Exod. 28:2, 40). He brings you and me and all believers to the glory of heaven. He consecrates Himself and establishes His credentials as High Priest forever; the verb in verse 10, "make perfect," being the same as used for the priest's consecration (in Exod. 29 and Lev. 4:5; 8:33; 16:32; 21:10). He washes us clean, sanctifying and consecrating us so we can freely enter His holy presence. He identifies Himself with us and calls us "brothers" or part of the family. That is the power of suffering. Do you want to be part of it? Be faithful to Jesus.

The Power over Death (5:14–18)

Does Jesus really understand us? Is His suffering really like my suffering? Look at the facts. He did not stay in heaven. He came to earth. He did not maintain royal, divine prerogatives. He left heaven's power for earth's poverty. He became a flesh-and-blood person like you and me. No, He did not become an angel. He became a person. Why? He faced an enemy: death. Victory could come only on the enemy's territory: the grave. Jesus suffered death, a horrible, gruesome death. Why? To defeat death forever. Resurrection is the victory over death, but resurrection comes only when one dies. Jesus knew how much you feared death. He knew how final death appears to you. He did not want you to live a life in fear. He defeated death to give you hope. He solved the sin problem. How? He faced every temptation you can face but never gave in. He never sinned. Thus He was perfect. Being perfect, He became the sacrificial lamb. He made salvation possible. He became our Savior. Is He your Savior?

■ TRUTHS TO LIVE BY

Power lies in your hands. God delegated responsibility for His creation to you. How are you using the power? In creative ways? or in sinful ways?

Power to save comes through suffering and death. Power does not come from personal achievement. Power comes by defeating the enemy on enemy territory. You must recognize that the real enemy is death and the prince of death. That is one enemy you alone will never have power to defeat. Thus God sent His Son Jesus with power to win the victory. He won through suffering and death. He died only to be raised from death. Do you have resurrection hope? Trust His power.

Power belongs to the Savior. Jesus has all power, the very power of God. He gave it up once to become a person like you and me and win victory over death. This brought Him the eternal crown of glory, eternal power over all creation. Do you depend on Him for power?

A VERSE TO REMEMBER

But we see Jesus, who was made a little lower than the angels for the suffering of death, crowned with glory and honour; that he by the grace of God should taste death for every man.—Hebrews 2:9

DAILY BIBLE READINGS

July 7 — Jesus Christ Gives Eternal Life. John 10:22–30
July 8 — Jesus Christ Is of God. 1 John 4:1–6
July 9 — Jesus Christ Is Love. 1 John 4:7–12
July 10 — Jesus Christ Resisted Temptations. Matt. 4:1–11
July 11 — Jesus Christ Was Sent by God. John 3:16–21
July 12 — Jesus Christ, Our Advocate. 1 John 2:1–6
July 13 — Jesus Christ Was Faithful. Heb. 3:1–6

Jesus Is the High Priest

Hebrews 4:14—5:10

Paul meant so much to me. He was a seminary student. He came from out of state. He did not have a lot of money. He knew how to work hard. He had suffered in life's hard-knocks school. He liked Old Testament studies. He was just like me in so many ways. I could talk to Paul in ways I had never talked to anyone else. Paul was like me enough that he understood me and could help me. That is the kind of person I can go to for help. That is the kind of person Jesus is.

■ THE BIBLE LESSON

14 Seeing then that we have a great high priest, that is passed into the heavens, Jesus the Son of God, let us hold fast our profession.

15 For we have not an high priest which cannot be touched with the feeling of our infirmities; but was in all points tempted like as we are, yet without sin.

16 Let us therefore come boldly unto the throne of grace, that we may obtain mercy, and find grace to help in time of need.

....

1 For every high priest taken from among men is ordained for men in things pertaining to God, that he may offer both gifts and sacrifices for sins:

2 Who can have compassion on the ignorant, and on them that are out of the way; for that he himself also is compassed with infirmity.

3 And by reason hereof he ought, as for the people, so also for himself, to offer for sins.

4 And no man taketh this honour unto himself, but he that is called of God, as was Aaron.

5 So also Christ glorified not himself to be made an high priest; but he that said unto him, Thou art my Son, to day have I begotten thee.

6 As he saith also in another place, Thou art a priest for ever after the order of Melchisedec.

7 Who in the days of his flesh, when he had offered up prayers and supplications with strong crying and tears unto him that was able to save him from death, and was heard in that he feared;

8 Though he were a Son, yet learned he obedience by the things which he suffered;

9 And being made perfect, he became the author of eternal salvation unto all them that obey him;

10 Called of God an high priest after the order of Melchisedec.

■ THE LESSON EXPLAINED

A Priest Who Understands Me (4:14–16)

Uncomfortable! This religious talk just makes me feel uneasy. I do not understand it. I need something I can touch and smell and see. Religion seems so unreal. Perhaps if we could go back to the Jewish system and see real smoke, hear real animals, smell real flesh and blood, inhale incense and perfume. Then we would be doing something real. Religion might come alive again.

You fear Jesus is not real? Look again. He came down from heaven. He endured every kind of situation you and I ever will endure, even the horrible death on the cross. He took children into His arms. He walked the streets homeless. He talked to down-and-out people who had sold their lives in professional sex. He was just the kind of person you and I would like to be. He was perfect.

So what? you ask. That means He is available to you right now. You can stride confidently into His presence and ask Him to forgive you and save you and love you. He will. You do not have to ask someone else to burn animals for you. You can talk to Jesus immediately. Whatever you need, He has the power and the love and the grace. He will help you.

A Priest Who Is Eternal (5:1–6)

This animal-burning system you like depends on men. We have to set apart some person to represent us before God and burn our sacrifices. Such a person should be able to show love and compassion, for he has to suffer just like we do. He is a man. In fact, so much a man he has to burn animals to get rid of his own sin. Fortunately, God shows us which men to choose, always men from the same family, Aaron's. Jesus is better. God chose Him, just like He chose Aaron. But He chose Him to be a Son, not just a priest, and to have an eternal priesthood. You know the story in Genesis 14 of Melchisedec, the priest who appeared from nowhere and disappeared to nowhere so that he seemed to be eternal. Well, Jesus is that kind of priest, only better. He is eternal. We never have to find out who is priest now. Jesus always is Priest.

A Priest Who Saves Forever (5:7–10)

What does Jesus do as Priest? What He did in His lifetime. His life was a continuous sacrifice to God, offering all He had in obedience, praying and talking to God continuously. God accepted this as the perfect life and the perfect offering. Thus as Priest, Jesus became the perfect source of salvation for you and me. What do we have to do? Give our lives to Jesus in total obedience, wanting to do whatever He says. Is that you?

■ TRUTHS TO LIVE BY

God expects you to be faithful. The faithful High Priest seeks faithful followers who obey Him.

God expects you to come to Him with boldness. Jesus shows you the way to God is clear. You can trust Him with any problem you have. He understands. He has experienced what you are experiencing. He wants to listen. Do not be afraid. Talk to God.

God expects you to accept Christ's salvation. Jesus did everything necessary for you to have eternal salvation. Will you let Him save you? Or must you have something you can touch?

■ A VERSE TO REMEMBER

Let us therefore come boldly unto the throne of grace, that we may obtain mercy, and find grace to help in time of need.—Hebrews 4:16

■ DAILY BIBLE READINGS

July 14 — Melchezedek Is King of Peace. Heb. 7:1-9
July 15 — High Priests Offer Blood Sacrifices. Heb. 9:1-10
July 16 — Christ's Prayer to Be Glorified. John 17:1-5
July 17 — Christ Is High Priest Forever. Heb. 7:10-19
July 18 — Christ Sits at God's Right Hand. Heb. 8:1-7
July 19 — Christ Intercedes for Us. Heb. 7:20-28
July 20 — Nothing Can Separate Us from God. Rom. 8:31-39

Jesus Is the Sacrifice

Hebrews 10:1–14

I let myself out of the building and walk into the street. Suddenly, fear absorbs my body. I want to run. No, I want to vanish. Why? I am the last person out of the building. A young black student is walking towards me. I picture all sorts of things this young man might do to me. I am afraid? Why? Because the young man is threatening me or has a history of chasing me? No! Never saw him before. I am afraid because he is black. Such fear is wrong. I know it is wrong. It is part of racial prejudice that I tell everyone I have overcome, but I have not. I am guilty of racial prejudice just at the moment I think I am free of it. What do I do with my guilt? I take it to a dark-skinned Carpenter from Galilee.

■ THE BIBLE LESSON

1 For the law having a shadow of good things to come, and not the very image of the things, can never with those sacrifices which they offered year by year continually make the comers thereunto perfect.

2 For then would they not have ceased to be offered? because that the worshippers once purged should have had no more conscience of sins.

3 But in those sacrifices there is a remembrance again made of sins every year.

4 For it is not possible that the blood of bulls and of goats should take away sins.

5 Wherefore when he cometh into the world, he saith, Sacrifice and offering thou wouldest not, but a body hast thou prepared me:

6 In burnt offerings and sacrifices for sin thou hast had no pleasure.

7 Then said I, Lo, I come (in the volume of the book it is written of me,) to do thy will, O God.

8 Above when he said, Sacrifice and offering and burnt offerings and offering for sin thou wouldest not, neither hadst pleasure therein; which are offered by the law;

9 Then said he, Lo, I come to do thy will, O God. He taketh away the first, that he may establish the second.

10 By the which will we are sanctified through the offering of the body of Jesus Christ once for all.

11 And every priest standeth daily ministering and offering oftentimes the same sacrifices, which can never take away sins:

12 But this man, after he had offered one sacrifice for sins for ever, sat down on the right hand of God;

13 From henceforth expecting till his enemies be made his footstool.

14 For by one offering he hath perfected for ever them that are sanctified.

■ THE LESSON EXPLAINED

Sacrifice Must Deal with Sin (10:1–4)

Burning animals and spreading perfume and incense all around has such a romantic ring to it. Just love to be part of it. Does seem odd though, that they keep doing the same thing over and over again. Why is that? Sacrifices, burning animals, are supposed to take care of our sin problem. But the act does not work right. Each time we sin, we need to have new sacrifices. The system keeps itself going forever and ever. Really, sacrifices just remind me that I have sinned and need help. They make me look for a better sacrifice that can really deal with sin. Certainly animals cannot do away with my sin. I need something better.

Sacrifice by Jesus Deals with Sin Forever (10:5–10)

The Old Testament prepared us to look for something better. Just look at Psalm 40:6–8; Isaiah 1:11; Jeremiah 6:20. When I look at the Greek translation (the Septuagint) of Psalm 40, I find what God expected. God prepared a human body for His Son to have to come into the world and be the perfect sacrifice that animals could not be. God knew the Son would say, I am willing to obey Your will. God planned all along to do away with the animal system for a better system, a Christ system. The Christ system has only one sacrifice made one time for all people forever.

Sacrifice by Jesus Makes You Holy (10:11–14)

Priests get into a routine. Offer sacrifice. Offer sacrifice again. Offer sacrifice again. On and on and on. Jesus broke the routine. He offered one sacrifice. It dealt with sins perfectly. Then He returned to His home in heaven with God. The Sacrifice became the eternal Savior at God's right hand. Now He waits for God's time for final victory over sin and Satan and death. He knows He has done all that is necessary. He has made it possible for us to be holy, totally dedicated to Him. We are what the sacrificial system tried but could not make us. We are fit for God's presence. We are forgiven. Guilt has no place in our lives. Does that describe you?

■ TRUTHS TO LIVE BY

Guilt is universal. All people deal with guilt because none live up to their own expectations, much less God's. You are not alone. Everyone is guilty.

Guilt has no human answer. Better job, better marriage, better finances, better therapist, better place to live . . . the search for an escape from guilt goes on. Nothing gives an answer.

Guilt has God's answer. God planned a way of escape, a way to lose your guilt once and forever. He sent Jesus as the perfect Sacrifice for sin after giving the sacrificial system so we could understand what Jesus was doing. You have no reason to be guilty. Jesus paid the price for your sin and guilt. Will you accept Him as your sacrifice?

■ A VERSE TO REMEMBER

For by one offering he hath perfected for ever them that are sanctified.—Hebrews 10:14

■ DAILY BIBLE READINGS

July 21 — Christ Sacrificed One Time Only. Heb. 9:23–28
July 22 — The New Covenant Superior to First. Heb. 8:8–13
July 23 — The New Covenant Verified. Heb. 9:11–22
July 24 — God Does Not Want Sacrifice. Ps. 40:4–10
July 25 — To Obey Is Better Than Sacrifice. 1 Sam. 15:17–23
July 26 — To Love Is Better Than Sacrifice. Mark 12:28–34
July 27 — Walk Humbly with Your God. Mic. 6:1–8

Grow in Faithfulness

Hebrews 5:11–6:10

Nine years old. First big job: fold the boxes in the bakery so the baker could put fresh cookies and pies in them. What a good feeling. I felt grown up, good about myself. Then a friend came by to buy a cake. The baker popped out a fresh batch of brownies from the oven. Talking and eating was more fun than folding boxes. My boss had to take me aside for some serious talking. Yes, Dad, I have learned my lesson. I will faithfully fold boxes every minute I am supposed to be at work. Nothing else will take my mind off the job. I will do what I am hired to do. Lesson was easy to learn and even to apply in the bakery. It is not so easy when God is the Father, and everything I do is in the field of learning.

■ THE BIBLE LESSON

11 Of whom we have many things to say, and hard to be uttered, seeing ye are dull of hearing.

12 For when for the time ye ought to be teachers, ye have need that one teach you again which be the first principles of the oracles of God; and are become such as have need of milk, and not of strong meat.

13 For every one that useth milk is unskilful in the word of righteousness: for he is a babe.

14 But strong meat belongeth to them that are of full age, even those who by reason of use have their senses exercised to discern both good and evil.

....

1 Therefore leaving the principles of the doctrine of Christ, let us go on unto perfection; not laying again the foundation of repentance from dead works, and of faith toward God,

2 Of the doctrine of baptisms, and of laying on of hands, and of resurrection of the dead, and of eternal judgment.

3 And this will we do, if God permit.

4 For it is impossible for those who were once enlightened, and have tasted of the heavenly gift, and were made partakers of the Holy Ghost,

5 And have tasted the good word of God, and the powers of the world to come,

6 If they shall fall away, to renew them again unto repentance; seeing they crucify to themselves the Son of God afresh, and put him to an open shame.

7 For the earth which drinketh in the rain that cometh oft upon it, and bringeth forth herbs meet for them by whom it is dressed, receiveth blessing from God:

8 But that which beareth thorns and briers is rejected, and is nigh unto cursing; whose end is to be burned.

9 But, beloved, we are persuaded better things of you, and things that accompany salvation, though we thus speak.

10 For God is not unrighteous to forget your work and labour of love, which ye have shewed toward his name, in that ye have ministered to the saints, and do minister.

THE LESSON EXPLAINED

Action, Not Advice (5:11-14)

Tired of hearing that. I have heard it before. I can say it as well as you can. Jesus died for me. I should live for Him every day. I should obey Him in everything I do. You are right. You know the lesson well. You want to be teacher, not pupil. One problem! Knowing is not enough. You must do what you know. Until then you are like a little child that we keep giving bottles of milk. Why? The child's stomach is not developed enough to eat meat and potatoes. Until you can take the lessons of the Bible and put them into daily practice, you remain a baby Christian. We have to tell you the same things over and over until not only can you repeat them back but also you can mirror them in daily actions. When you know good and evil and choose to do good, then you are mature, ready to teach others. Then I will not repeat the same lesson over and over again for you.

Progress, Not Regress (6:1–3)

The goal? You know it as well as I do. Perfection! Expect to do right every time. Yes, you are measured by action, not by doctrine. You have learned everything you need to know. You know what Jesus did. You know how to repent. You know you have to trust Jesus, not rely on something you have accomplished. You know ritual washings do nothing for you; even getting wet in baptism does not do the job. You know the true teaching of resurrection hope based on Jesus' resurrection. You know who faces eternal judgment and why. Quit going backwards and trying to learn something else. Go forwards. Become perfect like God wants you to. Obey Him!

Expectation, Not Condemnation (6:4–12)

Sounds so complicated. It is not. You know the Jewish system: Do things over and over again. Sin, repent, sacrifice. Sin, repent, sacrifice. That does not work with Jesus. You do not take Jesus today, give Him up tomorrow, get Him again day after tomorrow. Jesus is serious. He wants you to choose His way and stay in that way. He wants more than head knowledge. He wants heart knowledge and foot action. You cannot expect Jesus to go back to the Cross every time you change your mind. This is not a play-it-again-Sam kind of thing. This is the serious situation of God's way of salvation. There is only one way, the "Jesus Christ died for our sins once and for all" way. Express your faith once and for all and get on with the job of obeying Jesus. I know we have given you harsh words, hard to take. Do not worry. We just want you to realize how serious all this is. We expect good things from you. You chose the Jesus way. You will stay with it. We expect to see His salvation show itself in your daily life. We know the good things you have done for God. We expect you to keep on and do even greater things for Him.

■ TRUTHS TO LIVE BY

Faithfulness is more than knowledge. Jesus did not come to teach you knowledge to give to others. He came to give you a life to live before others. Take a spiritual inventory. Are you obeying what you know, or are you proud of teaching others what you yourself refuse to put into action. Faithfulness is doing the truth.

Faithfulness leads to greater obedience. Faithfulness is not a repeated routine. Faithfulness is a pathway of growth with greater obedience, greater faith, and greater understanding each day. Faithfulness sets the goal of perfection and marches to it.

Faithfulness displays salvation. Faithfulness does not repeat arguments about doctrines or take credit because I know more than you know. Faithfulness does not have an excuse to sin and expect God to take care of it. Faithfulness does not come one day and leave the next. Faithfulness shows you the life of Jesus in human flesh, day by day. Faithfulness proves Jesus saves.

■ A VERSE TO REMEMBER

Therefore leaving the principles of the doctrine of Christ, let us go on unto perfection.—Hebrews 6:1

■ DAILY BIBLE READINGS

July 28 — God's Covenant Promise Unchanged. Heb. 6:12–30
July 29 — Servants Rewarded for Good Work. Matt. 10:34–42
July 30 — By Grace We Are Saved. Eph. 2:1–8
July 31 — Escape Temptations with God's Help. 1 Cor. 10:1–13
August 1 — God Punishes the Wicked. Job 4:1–9
August 2 — Grow Up to Your Salvation. 1 Pet. 2:1–10
August 3 — Prophecy Comes from the Holy Spirit. 2 Pet. 1:12–21

Remain Near to God

Hebrews 10:19–39

Hide and seek. The name still brings fond memories, especially of times when we played in the coach's backyard next door. There we always tried to find new places to hide and a new way to sneak around until we could get to home base. Surprising how many different ways you can find to do things in one small yard. Guess I am still like that, looking for ways to do things differently. Problem is, I want to find different ways to God, too. How many ways does He have?

■ THE BIBLE LESSON

19 Having therefore, brethren, boldness to enter into the holiest by the blood of Jesus,

20 By a new and living way, which he hath consecrated for us, through the veil, that is to say, his flesh;

21 And having an high priest over the house of God;

22 Let us draw near with a true heart in full assurance of faith, having our hearts sprinkled from an evil conscience, and our bodies washed with pure water.

23 Let us hold fast the profession of our faith without wavering; (for he is faithful that promised;)

24 And let us consider one another to provoke unto love and to good works:

25 Not forsaking the assembling of ourselves together, as the manner of some is; but exhorting one another: and so much the more, as ye see the day approaching.

. . . .

32 But call to remembrance the former days, in which, after ye were illuminated, ye endured a great fight of afflictions;

33 Partly, whilst ye were made a gazingstock both by reproaches and afflictions; and partly, whilst ye became companions of them that were so used.

34 For ye had compassion of me in my bonds, and took joyfully the spoiling of your goods, knowing in yourselves that ye have in heaven a better and an enduring substance.

35 Cast not away therefore your confidence, which hath great recompence of reward.

36 For ye have need of patience, that, after ye have done the will of God, ye might receive the promise.

37 For yet a little while, and he that shall come will come, and will not tarry.

38 Now the just shall live by faith: but if any man draw back, my soul shall have no pleasure in him.

39 But we are not of them who draw back unto perdition; but of them that believe to the saving of the soul.

THE LESSON EXPLAINED

One Way (10:19–23)

Why sneak around looking for new ways to get there, when the entrance is clearly marked? On the cross, Jesus opened the way to God. He removed the fear. No longer is God in a temple with barriers up so that only one person one time a year can enter into God's living place. Jesus' blood takes away your sins. Jesus' blood makes you clean and pure and holy. Jesus' blood makes you qualified to enter God's holy presence. Jesus is the Priest who is welcome in God's presence every day. Jesus wants to take you with Him as He enters the Father's living quarters. Come on, let's go with Him. No reason for doubts and fears. Jesus is with us.

One Walk (10:24–31)

What does it mean to be near God? It means to be like God, to have His love, His care, His purity, His power. It means to walk every day consistently, just as Jesus did.

Help other people. Minister to their needs. Put them before your own selfish needs. Worship together in God's presence. Encourage one another. Quit choosing to sin. Choose to obey. Have confidence that when Judgment Day comes, you will still remain near to God. But what will happen if you have all the opportunity you have had and then decide to go a different direction? Do not fool yourself. God's judgment is real, and you do not want to experience it. No need to. Go with Jesus into His presence. Stay close to Him.

One Winner (10:32–39)

How can I do that? Look backwards. Remember what you have been through with Jesus. No, better phrased, remember what Jesus has been through with you. Others laughed and made fun of you. Still you found joy in ministry and obeying Jesus. You remained convinced that Jesus would give you rewards in heaven. Why lose confidence now? Jesus is the same. He will take you into God's presence now and for eternity. Just be patient a little longer. Endure the problems you face a little stronger. Jesus made the promise. He will keep the promise. You will receive the promise. He is coming again. You can count on that. Then you will be near God forever. You have to choose. Two sides fight day by day: Satan's side and God's side. Where do you stand? I have confidence. You are on God's side. Stick with us just a bit longer. Jesus is coming again. Stay close to Him.

■ TRUTHS TO LIVE BY

Jesus' way is the only way to be close to God. Quit thinking you will find a happier road and a better life. Jesus on the cross showed that suffering is necessary in this life, but the hope of heaven makes it all worthwhile. Patiently walk His way, and look for the promise.

Jesus' way is a walk of love with others. No solo performances on this road. Stay with His church. Minister in His name. Let love flow through you every day. Then fear of judgment vanishes. God's nearness hides all fears and doubts.

Jesus' way is certain. He promised. He will come again. You can trust Him in a way you can trust no one else. Stay on Jesus' way. Looking for any other is foolish. Just quietly, faithfully, patiently walk with Jesus until the promise is complete.

■ A VERSE TO REMEMBER

Let us hold fast the profession of our faith without wavering; (for he is faithful that promised).—Hebrews 10:23

■ DAILY BIBLE READINGS

August 4— Power Belongs to God. 2 Cor. 4:7–12
August 5— Be Born of the Holy Spirit. John 3:1–15
August 6— Things of the Spirit Are Unseen. 2 Cor. 4:13–18
August 7— Jesus' Prayer for the Church. John 17:20–26
August 8— God Speaks Through His Word. Ps. 19:7–14
August 9— A Genuine Faith Is Important. 1 Pet. 1:3–9
August 10— God Is Faithful. 1 Cor. 1:1–10

Remember the Past

Hebrews 11:1–40

"Ph.D., published writer, experienced editor, university professor, good preacher, unemployed." Many qualified young men and women fit this description today when we have trained more people than we have jobs for. How do you react in this situation? With anger? Hurt? Frustration? Uncertainty? Self-doubt? Fear? All of these enter the picture. Many people, however, react with heroism. They join the roll call of faith from Hebrews 11 as they search out new opportunities and trust in God through hard times.

■ THE BIBLE LESSON

1 Now faith is the substance of things hoped for, the evidence of things not seen.

2 For by it the elders obtained a good report.

....

6 But without faith it is impossible to please him: for he that cometh to God must believe that he is, and that he is a rewarder of them that diligently seek him.

7 By faith Noah, being warned of God of things not seen as yet, moved with fear, prepared an ark to the saving of his house; by the which he condemned the world, and became heir of the righteousness which is by faith.

8 By faith Abraham, when he was called to go out into a place which he should after receive for an inheritance, obeyed; and he went out, not knowing whither he went.

9 By faith he sojourned in the land of promise, as in a strange country, dwelling in tabernacles with Isaac and Jacob, the heirs with him of the same promise:

10 For he looked for a city which hath foundations, whose builder and maker is God.

....

13 These all died in faith, not having received the promises, but having seen them afar off, and were persuaded of them, and embraced them, and confessed that they were strangers and pilgrims on the earth.

14 For they that say such things declare plainly that they seek a country.

15 And truly, if they had been mindful of that country from whence they came out, they might have had opportunity to have returned.

16 But now they desire a better country, that is, an heavenly: wherefore God is not ashamed to be called their God: for he hath prepared for them a city.

. . . .

39 And these all, having obtained a good report through faith, received not the promise:

40 God having provided some better thing for us, that they without us should not be made perfect.

■ THE LESSON EXPLAINED

Faith Defined (11:1–6)

"You keep hammering the point home: you must be faithful no matter what. Hold on to Jesus in faith despite all circumstances. One question? What do you mean by faith?" Glad you asked. Faith gives content to your dreams. It guarantees you will receive what you cannot see. It is the criterion God used to judge our ancestors as acceptable to Him. Faith is trusting so much in what you have been promised that you act like you have received the promise already without any visible evidence that you have. Faith is living as though you are in heaven while you are still on earth. Faith is believing God exists and has done everything the Bible says He has. Faith is knowing Jesus Christ has saved you for now and eternity. Faith is the only way you can please God. How is your faith supply?

Faith in Person (11:7-38)

Sound impossible or foolish to trust something you cannot see? Look at some people. They have been very visible on this earth. God told Noah a flood was coming. In faith Noah built a boat on dry land, not just any boat but the boat God commanded to be built to save the animals and his family. God told Abram to leave his kindred and his homeland to take a journey with no known destination. Abram moved his family. God told him when to stop. Abram never saw God's final promise. He never lived in God's city. Abram never owned the land. Still the nation Israel resulted. Abram, renamed Abraham, is the father of your faith.

Notice carefully Abraham's faith. He, his son, and his grandson all died without possessing the land. Even in death they remained convinced: they would receive the promise. They confessed this faith openly to all who would listen. They never let their thoughts dwell on what they missed, what they left, what might have been. They looked forward to what God promised. God did not let them down. He has a heavenly reward for them and gladly claims them as His people, members of His family.

The list goes on and on. Think about each name on the list. All lived in faith. All acted on God's command, even when they did not get what they wanted immediately. Most suffered greatly. Still they believed. And you?

Faith in Waiting (11:39-40)

The roll call of faith ends. The heroes stand before us, examples we admire. They have widely different stories. They share one thing: no one received the promise. Why? God waited for the perfect moment in His perfect plan of salvation. He waited for us, for you and me, to participate in Christ. These great heroes of faith could not get their final reward until God used us to show the perfect promise in Christ. Only when God in Christ perfectly did away with sin was the promise ready for completion. All are ready to receive the same reward together: the reward of eternal life in Christ. Do you have faith you have received eternal life?

TRUTHS TO LIVE BY

Faith accepts without seeing. Life holds more than what the test tube can prove. Life centers on the invisible God and your love relationship with Him. Faith believes God has provided salvation even when life's daily experience does not look like salvation.

Faith sees future promises, not past opportunities. Faith looks forward, knowing God will deliver what He promised. Faith refuses to look backward to wish for good old days and opportunities slipped by.

Faith feeds on examples. Faith joins a multitude whose faith lasted until death. Their experiences encourage us to keep the faith until God brings the reward.

Faith knows salvation. Faith waits for heaven but does so in possession of God's gift in grace of salvation. Christ has died and solved the sin problem. His resurrection gives hope. His salvation changes life now.

A VERSE TO REMEMBER

Now faith is the substance of things hoped for, the evidence of things not seen.—Hebrews 11:1

DAILY BIBLE READINGS

August 11 — The Faith of Abraham. Heb. 11:17–22
August 12 — The Faith of Moses. Heb. 11:23–28
August 13 — The Faith of the Israelites. Heb. 11:29–38
August 14 — Abraham Gave God the Glory. Rom. 4:13–20
August 15 — God's Promise to Abraham. Gal. 3:15–22
August 16 — Righteousness Comes Through Faith. Rom. 9:27–33
August 17 — Faith Without Works Is Dead. James 2:18–26

Renew Commitment

Hebrews 12:1–11

Lindsay could not believe it. His beautiful wife of so many years came in, sat down, and said, "Call the doctor." Before the doctor could come the few short blocks, she was dead. I could not believe the news, either. Lindsay is one of the cloud of witnesses to faith that I have depended on for so long. As a young youth minister and then pastor, I watched this layman keep a church together in difficult times and from him I learned how to renew enthusiasm and commitment when all signs said, Quit. As I pray for Lindsay in his loss, I commit myself anew to the Lord whom Lindsay and his beautiful family have served so faithfully.

■ THE BIBLE LESSON

1 Wherefore seeing we also are compassed about with so great a cloud of witnesses, let us lay aside every weight, and the sin which doth so easily beset us, and let us run with patience the race that is set before us,

2 Looking unto Jesus the author and finisher of our faith; who for the joy that was set before him endured the cross, despising the shame, and is set down at the right hand of the throne of God.

3 For consider him that endured such contradiction of sinners against himself, lest ye be wearied and faint in your minds.

4 Ye have not yet resisted unto blood, striving against sin.

5 And ye have forgotten the exhortation which speaketh unto you as unto children, My son, despise not thou the chastening of the Lord, nor faint when thou art rebuked of him:

6 For whom the Lord loveth he chasteneth, and scourgeth every son whom he receiveth.

7 If ye endure chastening, God dealeth with you as with sons; for what son is he whom the father chasteneth not?

8 But if ye be without chastisement, whereof all are partakers, then are ye bastards, and not sons.

9 Furthermore we have had fathers of our flesh which corrected us, and we gave them reverence: shall we not much rather be in subjection unto the Father of spirits, and live?

10 For they verily for a few days chastened us after their own pleasure; but he for our profit, that we might be partakers of his holiness.

11 Now no chastening for the present seemeth to be joyous, but grievous: nevertheless afterward it yieldeth the peaceable fruit of righteousness unto them which are exercised thereby.

■ THE LESSON EXPLAINED

Commitment to Quit Sinning (12:1-4)

Overwhelmed by the roll call of faith? What do you do with it? Let the names encourage you. They are the witnesses clouding and crowding around you. Keep on. It is worth the struggle. Run the race as hard and fast as you can. Do not let the world tie weights onto your legs so that you cannot run fast enough. Do not let Satan lure you into sin that makes you detour off course. Do not be frustrated that you are in a marathon and not a dash. Be patient. You will see the finish line. You will win the victory. How? By keeping your eyes on the goal, on Jesus Christ Himself. He finished the race perfectly and waits at the finish line to greet you and give you the crown of victory. Yes, the race was as hard for Him as it is for you, even harder. Have you suffered on a cross yet? He is beside God on the throne. Have sinners done to you what they did to Jesus, crucifying Him even though it meant punishment for them? If Jesus can endure all that, are you going to give up? Commit yourself anew and afresh to the race. You are not too tired to run. Sin does not have dominion over you. Do not let it. Fight sin until your very last breath. Win the race.

Commitment in Response to Discipline (12:5–9)

Yes, the race is hard. Why? you want to know. Part of the answer is God. He does not want you to get off track. He disciplines you when you do. He loves you so much, He wants you to win. The only way to win is to stay on track, so He punishes you as you veer off course. All this means is that you are God's child, and He treats and loves you like a child. How do you react when your parent disciplines you? Should you not love, respect, and obey your Heavenly Father even more?

Commitment to Peace and Righteousness (12:10–11)

Why accept such discipline? you ask. Because it is from God. It is not like your parents, who sometimes made mistakes and disciplined you for things you did not do. God is perfect. He disciplines only when necessary and in ways that help you. He keeps you on the path of holiness, the path away from sin. It hurts. I know it does. Nobody enjoys and celebrates being punished. But look at the results. God's discipline makes sure you stay on course and win the race. It gives you peace of mind and spirit as you run. It lets you do what is right and fair and just. It puts you in the frame of mind and on the course of action you will experience and follow in heaven. Commitment to Christ's race means you will receive these prizes from Him. Can you endure?

■ TRUTHS TO LIVE BY

Commitment has a goal. Christian commitment is not a meaningless path through ritual and meetings. It is a determination to be what Christ wants you to be, to become the person of faith that will inspire others. Commitment points you to a goal: be like Christ, living without sin so you can be with Christ in heaven.

Commitment has a hero. Jesus is the Christian's hero. Jesus has run the race to perfection. No one could do better. He has received His prize: sitting with God on the heavenly throne. This hero is the role model for you. Commit yourself to be like Him.

Commitment has a price. Victory never comes easy. You must train and discipline yourself. You must listen to coaching and follow it. You must suffer the consequences when you break training. You must endure the "boos" from opposition crowds. Christian commitment often brings horrible suffering. Paying the price is the only way to win the race.

■ A VERSE TO REMEMBER

Wherefore seeing we also are compassed about with so great a cloud of witnesses, let us lay aside every weight, and the sin which doth so easily beset us, and let us run with patience the race that is set before us.—Hebrews 12:1

■ DAILY BIBLE READINGS

August 18 — Be Committed to Peace. James 3:13–18
August 19 — In All Things Exercise Self Control. 1 Cor. 9:19–27
August 20 — Look to God for Wisdom. James 1:1–11
August 21 — Every Good Gift Is from God. James 1:12–18
August 22 — Act Out Your Beliefs. James 1:19–26
August 23 — Trust in the Lord. Prov. 3:1–12
August 24 — Pray for Renewal. Ps. 51

Accept Responsibilities

Hebrews 13:1–16

It's not my fault. He made me do it.
You knew better, didn't you?
Well, yes, but he is bigger than I am.
Did you have to do what he told you to?
He would have hurt me if I didn't.

How does a parent ever win an argument with a child? Still, I cannot give up trying to teach personal responsibility to each one of them. It is a hard lesson to teach. I keep having to learn it myself. I find myself telling others almost the same things the children used to tell me. I keep finding it hard to accept present discipline and revenge from others so that I can be true to my God and look forward in faith to His rewards.

THE BIBLE LESSON

1 Let brotherly love continue.

2 Be not forgetful to entertain strangers: for thereby some have entertained angels unawares.

3 Remember them that are in bonds, as bound with them; and them which suffer adversity, as being yourselves also in the body.

4 Marriage is honourable in all, and the bed undefiled: but whoremongers and adulterers God will judge.

5 Let your conversation be without covetousness; and be content with such things as ye have: for he hath said, I will never leave thee, nor forsake thee.

6 So that we may boldly say, The Lord is my helper, and I will not fear what man shall do unto me.

7 Remember them which have the rule over you, who have spoken unto you the word of God: whose faith follow, considering the end of their conversation.

8 Jesus Christ the same yesterday, and to day, and for ever.

9 Be not carried about with divers and strange doctrines. For it is a good thing that the heart be established with grace; not with meats, which have not profited them that have been occupied therein.

10 We have an altar, whereof they have no right to eat which serve the tabernacle.

11 For the bodies of those beasts, whose blood is brought into the sanctuary by the high priest for sin, are burned without the camp.

12 Wherefore Jesus also, that he might sanctify the people with his own blood, suffered without the gate.

13 Let us go forth therefore unto him without the camp, bearing his reproach.

14 For here have we no continuing city, but we seek one to come.

15 By him therefore let us offer the sacrifice of praise to God continually, that is, the fruit of our lips giving thanks to his name.

16 But to do good and to communicate forget not: for with such sacrifices God is well pleased.

■ THE LESSON EXPLAINED

Responsible to Love Others (13:1-6)

"Faith . . . the invisible . . . no evidence . . . cloud of witnesses . . . run the race . . . heavenly crown. Can you be more concrete? How does this all work out in real life?" It works out in a love relationship with God. Renewing your love to God each day leads you to show love to other people, especially God's people, even people you do not know. You remember Abraham's example in Genesis 18. He fed strangers and found they were God's angels. You show love to people even when helping them may put you in danger or cause you to be physically harmed. You display your love to the world by remaining faithful to your marriage vows. You know God judges and punishes those who let sexual urges control their lives. You display your love by giving to others instead of wanting what they have. You remain content with what you have, knowing God's presence is more important than anything you might own or control. Love proclaims trust in Christ and fearlessness before other people. Do not worry when someone threatens you harm. Trust God to carry you through, even if you must suffer.

Responsible to Obey Example of Leaders (13:7-8)

Love gains strength and guidance from the past. Leaders who created the church and planted God's Word in the church deserve respect and continued obedience. Why? Look at their lives even unto death. They have joined the heavenly cloud of witnesses because they were faithful. Be like them. Obey what they taught. Jesus is the same today as He was yesterday, and He will stay the same tomorrow. He rewarded your faithful leaders. He will reward you. Keep the faith they lived out before you. Love as they loved.

Responsible to Keep the Truth (13:9-12)

But other people have taken over. They preach exciting new things. They give me new freedom the old leaders said I could not have. They let me do what I have always wanted to try.

Is that the way of God's grace? Are these people better role models than the leaders faithful unto death? Do you really think that by choosing proper foods, giving thanks for them in the proper way, and then eating them together can bring you strength that you do not receive directly from God's grace? You know Jesus certainly did not obey ritual rules and interpretations. Why do you want to do so? Leaders taught you the truth. Keep it.

Responsible to Please God (13:13-16)

Yes, you have to change the way things are going. These new ways of doing things are wrong ways. We do not have a guaranteed ritual that lets us be certain we are saved because we participate in it. We have Christ's way of faith. Praise God for Christ and what Christ has done for us.

Through Him we know the final reward is ours. Through Him and Him only we have a daily love relationship with God. The love relationship leads us to do good to others and maintain the communication or fellowship within the church. This is the only way to please God.

TRUTHS TO LIVE BY

Faith in God results in acts of love for people. Faith does not lead us to hide ourselves together in secret rituals. It leads us to show love and kindness to one another. Faith assures us that we have salvation, so we do not try to keep on earning it. We share it.

Faith in God results in obedience. Faith does not lead us on a chase for freedom. It leads us on a race to obey God, refrain from sin, and be loyal to our family commitments. Faith does not seek material prosperity. It seeks citizenship in the heavenly city.

Faith in God clings to the unchanging Christ. Christ has shown us the depth of God's grace. We rely on Him and Him alone for salvation. The Word taught us that Christ is our guide, not new leaders with easier ways to be religious.

A VERSE TO REMEMBER

But to do good and to communicate forget not: for with such sacrifices God is well pleased.—Hebrews 13:16

DAILY BIBLE READINGS

August 25 — Be Responsible Husbands and Wives. Eph. 5:21–33

August 26 — Be Responsible Parents and Children. Eph. 6:1–9

August 27 — Be Responsible Citizens. Matt. 22:15–22

August 28 — Be Responsible to God. Heb. 4:1–10

August 29 — Be Responsible Leaders. Heb. 13:17–25

August 30 — Accept Responsibility for What You Say. James 3:1–12

August 31 — Use Your Wealth Responsibly. Luke 12:13–21

Respect for Human Life

Genesis 1:27; Matthew 5:13–16, 21–22, 27–28, 43–45

Tears filled her eyes. Ten years later the pain remained. The story flooded from her lips as though it were yesterday. Unwanted pregnancy. Seemingly no way out. Doctor advised abortion as the best solution to a horrible situation. In her youthful naiveté, she followed doctor's "orders." She has a name for the baby. She celebrates the baby's birthday. She expects to see the baby again in heaven. Meanwhile, the pain scorches her soul, not because the sin of the situation is not forgiven but because the human loss will never go away.

■ THE BIBLE LESSON

GENESIS 1

27 So God created man in his own image, in the image of God created he him; male and female created he them.

....

MATTHEW 5

13 Ye are the salt of the earth: but if the salt have lost his savor, wherewith shall it be salted? it is thenceforth good for nothing, but to be cast out, and to be trodden under foot of men.

14 Ye are the light of the world. A city that is set on an hill cannot be hid.

15 Neither do men light a candle, and put it under a bushel, but on a candlestick; and it giveth light unto all that are in the house.

16 Let your light so shine before men, that they may see your good works, and glorify your Father which is in heaven.

....

21 Ye have heard that it was said by them of old time, Thou shalt not kill; and whosoever shall kill shall be in danger of the judgment:

22 But I say unto you, That whosoever is angry with his brother without a cause shall be in danger of the judgment: and whosoever shall say to his brother, Raca, shall be in danger of the council: but whosoever shall say, Thou fool, shall be in danger of hell fire.

....

27 Ye have heard that it was said by them of old time, Thou shalt not commit adultery:

28 But I say unto you, That whosoever looketh on a woman to lust after her hath committed adultery with her already in his heart.

....

43 Ye have heard that it hath been said, Thou shalt love thy neighbour, and hate thine enemy.

44 But I say unto you, Love your enemies, bless them that curse you, do good to them that hate you, and pray for them which despitefully use you, and persecute you;

45 That ye may be the children of your Father which is in heaven.

■ THE LESSON EXPLAINED

The Source of Life (Gen. 1:27)

Life is precious. No one but God can create it. God gave it to us for a purpose. We have no right to abuse it. Rather God calls us to celebrate it as His very good, superlative, unmatched gift to us. The gift of life comes in two varieties: male and female. That means life has a sexual component. Sexual urges, sexual needs, sexual differences are part of God's creation. They belong, then, as part of the celebration of life. Everything involved in sex life should be able to be part of our celebration of God's goodness. Shame and guilt have no part in it. Life and all its components give us reason to praise God.

Role in Society (Matt. 5:13–16)

Life has zest. It has flavor. It contributes these qualities to society. Sadly, life can lose its zest and flavor. Life can become dull and boring. Why? How? Because life can be lived apart from the Source of life. Life apart from God is not life at all. It is living death. So many people live this way. Such deadly living gives reign to human atrocities such as freely killing young infants who have never seen the light of day. How can this be stopped? Only as believers are salt, giving such zest and flavor to life that others want what believers obviously have. When believers become the source of envy rather than hatred and scorn, then they can season the world with life. Then all the world will celebrate life's joy and praise life's Creator.

Value of Human Life (Matt. 5:21-22)

Killing and abortion are not the root issues. The human heart is the real problem. As long as life cannot be celebrated, dark, angry, vicious thoughts plague the human heart. Such thoughts destroy human relationships, set us free to hate and call other people names, and make us forget the value in every human life even when the life is not what we would want it to be. Such thoughts give rise to crimes of murder, passion, and abortion.

Purity in Human Relationships (Matt. 5:27-28)

Where does abortion begin? It begins in human lust, most often lust uncontrolled by any sense of value for human life. Such lust leads a person to use another person to fulfill lust rather than to show love for the other person. Lust makes one lose control of reason and conscience. Lust leads to sex without love, without caution, and without commitment of marriage. Such lust often leads to pregnancy, unexpected and unwanted. Training the eye not to look and the emotions not to lust is a major step on the road to valuing and celebrating life.

Respect in Action (Matt. 5:43-45*a*)

Celebrating life means celebrating people you do not agree with and do not like. Jesus ate with sinners, talked with prostitutes, and forgave those who betrayed or denied Him. Believers cannot condone sinful action, especially action that shows no value for life and is willing to kill the innocent, the unborn child. But how does the believer respond to such people, by killing in return? Jesus says,

Love your enemies. Pray for them. Do good to them. Helping the hated may be the extreme example of celebrating life and praising the Source of life.

TRUTHS TO LIVE BY

Life is reason to celebrate, not to despair. Every life God brings to the world is reason for celebration and protection. When God gives life, we have no excuse for taking life. We must find God's way to take care of life and celebrate.

Life goes bad when hearts go bad. God's gift of life always has potential to be very good. The human heart, controlled by sin and temptation, finds ways to hassle life, hate life, and hurt life. No unborn life can be bad. We have no right to condemn a new life because we have let sin make our life bad.

Life with seasoning can make even bad lives worth living. The believer seasons the world with celebration and salvation. Bad lives take notice of such seasoning and want it for themselves. When life is full of joy and daily practice shows love to the worst of people, the seasoning process has begun. Bad lives seasoned with Christ's love can be redeemed.

A VERSE TO REMEMBER

So God created man in his own image, in the image of God created he him; male and female created he them.
—Genesis 1:27

DAILY BIBLE READINGS

Jan. 13 — The Calling of Simon Peter. Mark 1:14–20
Jan. 14 — Peter's Pentecost Sermon. Acts 2:14–20
Jan. 15 — Peter Confirms Jesus' Resurrection. Acts 2:22–36
Jan. 16 — Peter Raised Two Persons from the Dead. Acts 9:32–42
Jan. 17 — Peter's Vision of Food. Acts 10:9–16
Jan. 18 — Peter Visits Cornelius. Acts 10:17–23
Jan. 19 — Peter's Sermon to Cornelius. Acts 10:34–43